Inter-regional Co-operation in the Social Sciences

unesco

ISBN 92-3-101500-1
French edition 92-3-201500-5

Published in 1977
by the United Nations Educational,
Scientific and Cultural Organization

Composed and printed in
the workshops of Unesco

Contents

Preface

The present issue of the Reports and Papers in the Social Sciences is devoted to the examination of the questions relating to the inter-regional co-operation in the social sciences based on the discussions of and working papers presented to an international meeting on the same subject convened by Unesco in Paris from 23 to 27 August 1976.

The meeting was convened in pursuance of resolution 3.211 adopted by the General Conference of Unesco at its eighteenth session which, among other things, authorized the Director-General "to encourage the institutional and organizational development of the social sciences, especially in the developing countries, by simulating regional and inter-regional co-ordination".

The meeting took stock of the current state of the social sciences in various regions and examined and suggested ways of strengthening international co-operation in the social sciences - as the reader will find in the final report of the meeting which is the first chapter of this volume.

All the participants were concerned with the development of the social sciences; both in terms of building up the infrastructures such as university departments, research institutes, and professional bodies on the one hand, and in terms of advancing the social sciences as a set of academic disciplines on the other. They were all keenly interested in enhancing the contributions the social sciences can make to the improvement of the human condition, particularly in the developing countries.

Unesco has continuously taken a very keen interest in the institutional development of the social sciences. A number of international professional associations came into being in the late 1940's and the early 1950's at Unesco's initiative and with its support. In Asia, a regional social science research centre was established in India in 1956 which conducted a series of research and training in the social sciences until it merged with an Indian institution in 1967. In Latin America, Unesco was instrumental in establishing in 1958 the Latin American Faculty of Social Sciences (FLACSO) and the Latin American Centre for Social Sciences (CENTRO). Unesco assisted the creation of two regional social science centres in the past few years in Africa and in the Arab region. The Secretariat has also been in close co-operation with regional social science bodies such as the Latin American Social Science Council (CLACSO), the Association of Asian Social Science Research Councils (AASSREC) and the Council for the Development of Economic and Social Research in Africa (CODESRIA).

It is on the basis of activities and experiences at regional levels that a new project aiming specifically at promoting inter-regional or global co-operation was conceived. The meeting marked the beginning of its implementation and helped largely determine its future course and content.

The views expressed are those of the authors and not necessarily those of Unesco.

CHAPTER 1

Inter-regional Co-operation in the Social Sciences: Final Report of the Meeting
Unesco, Paris, 23-27 August 1976

I. INTRODUCTION

1. Organization

(1) The General Conference of Unesco at its eighteenth session adopted resolution 3. 211 which among other things authorized the Director-General "to encourage the institutional and organizational development of the social sciences, especially in the developing countries, by stimulating regional and inter-regional co-ordination".

(2) The purpose of the meeting was to:

(i) examine critically the present state of social sciences in various regions;
(ii) define common problems and identify differences with regard to needs and priorities in the field of social science co-operation at regional and international levels;
(iii) investigate ways and means of strengthening international co-operation among social science institutions within and between regions; and
(iv) make specific recommendations for strengthening inter-regional collaboration.
(See Appendix 1, Programme)

(3) Eight participants who took part in the meeting were representatives of international or regional social science centres and associations. One participant from North America who was preparing a paper recently passed away, which resulted in non-representation of the region. There were also eight observers including a United Nations institute, and a regional intergovernmental body. (See Appendix 2, List of participants.)

(4) Seven working papers were presented and discussed at the meeting. (See Appendix 3. List of meeting documents.)

2. Opening session

(5) The meeting was officially opened by Dr. (Mrs. M. Hildebrandt, Assistant Director-General for the Sector of Social Sciences and their Applications. After explaining the general frame of reference for the meeting, she stressed the importance of developing the social sciences both in terms of building up infrastructures on the one hand and in terms of advancing the social sciences as a set of academic disciplines on the other. She further said that, by so doing, the social sciences could make greater contributions for the improvement of the human condition, especially in the developing countries.

(6) Dr. V. Mshvenieradze, Director of the Division for International Development of Social Sciences, welcomed the participants and observers. He briefly discussed the experience of the social science programmes of Unesco, which would soon celebrate its thirtieth anniversary. He introduced the staff members of the Division who took part in the meeting. Self-introductions were made by all the participants. A tribute was paid to the memory of the late Dr. Kalman Silvert, of the Ford Foundation, who had undertaken the preparation of a working paper concerning North America.

3. Election of officers

(7) The meeting elected unanimously the following officers:

Chairman:	Professor A. Bujra (CODESRIA)
Vice-Chairmen:	Professor A. Schaff (Vienna Centre)
	Dr. F. Delich (CLACSO)
Rapporteur:	Professor T. N. Madan (Asian Research Centre, Institute of Economic Growth)

II. SUMMARY OF DISCUSSIONS

1. Present state of the social sciences in different regions (Africa, Arab region, Asia, Europe, Latin America)

(8) It was clear from the papers presented at the meeting, and even more so from the ensuing

discussions, that, despite the far-flung nature of the regions, there were certain basic similarities characterizing the present state of social sciences in the Third World. Indeed, what was remarkable in this context was the extent to which the European region also shared some of the characteristics of the other regions. Thus it turned out that social science teaching and research anywhere in the world is more or less dependent upon what is going on in these fields in some other country or region. While Asian and African social scientists seem to be dependent upon European, and increasingly also, American social science tradition, Latin American and European social scientists apparently are linked to social sciences in North America. It is a pity that, owing to the sad and untimely demise of Professor Kalman Silvert, no paper dealing with the North American situation was available to the meeting, for it might well have emphasized the indebtedness of social sciences there to the past achievements and the present concerns of European social scientists. It is not merely the fact of a linkage that is noteworthy, but more so the fact that in the case of the developing regions, it is a relationship of dependency: to put it in other words (repeatedly used at the meeting), it is a "vertical" relationship, between donors and recipients, between patrons and clients.

(9) Social sciences in the Third World countries have emerged and then grown or, if one prefers, become staltified, in the setting of colonialism. The apparently innocent fact-finding studies of foreign social scientists in the colonies served the purpose of colonial administrators in one form or another. Though practically all the Third World countries are now politically independent, "self-rule" in the field of social sciences remains still to be achieved. Educational and research institutions, old and new, are modelled on European, British or American originals: there has been a quantitative expansion of education and research but hardly any qualitative change in their purpose as evidenced by outdated and irrelevant curricula; the numbers of indigenous social scientists have undoubtedly increased but they are more in contact with their Western colleagues than with their counterparts in the Third World or, for that matter, even within their own region; the questions these social scientists ask, the paradigms and research techniques they employ, the vision they have of the future of their countries - all these are for the most part imported from the West, or at best adapted from the work of Western thinkers including social scientists. No wonder, then, that social sciences in the Third World are often judged to be irrelevant and the social scientists accused of being alienated from their societies.

(10) It would be, however, a mistake to take a totally negative view of this "vertical" relationship. Even the colonial administrator has left behind him data of considerable value for a relevant social science - for example census materials or surveys of natural resources. Also, the volume of available work on which to build is often very largely determined by the interest which foreign social scientists, and the "natives" trained by them, have taken in a country. It is clear that many countries which escaped colonization (e. g. Afghanistan, Nepal and Thailand in Asia) also took longer to evolve modern educational systems and have remained particularly weak in the field of social sciences. The point, then, is not that all past work has to be set aside but that it has to be critically evaluated in the light of today's needs. Similarly, the point is not that only local scholars will engage in social science research in a country but that the total co-operative endeavour will serve national goals. Such a satisfactory state of teaching and research in the social sciences has yet to be achieved in the Third World countries but they certainly are on the road leading to it. There is clear recognition of and enthusiasm for intraregional co-operation in determining priorities in research and conducting it. This was clearly demonstrated, for instance, by the success of the Unesco/CERDAS missions of 1975 and 1976 in Africa.

(11) A general characteristic of social sciences in all the regions turned out to be the unsatisfactory character of "horizontal" relations between the countries of each region. A major reason for this, it seems, is the fact that not all countries in a region (and this is as true of Europe as of, say, Africa) have attained the same level of development in this field. The question that faces each country, whatever the level of development of social sciences in it, is twofold: first, what kind of social sciences it wants - that is, for what purpose? And two, whether it can develop these in isolation? The answer to the first question would seem to be that social sciences have to solve social problems - that they have to be nationally relevant. The answer to the second is equally clear: social sciences can best be developed through co-operative endeavour, pooling the experience and resources - for both are yet limited - of countries and of regions.

(12) Some other characteristics of the social sciences in the Third World which are typical of some regions but not of others were also discussed. Thus the phenomenon of internal brain drain within the Arab region was mentioned. It seems that many social scientists there have chosen to pursue material advantage rather than participate in the developmental efforts of their own countries. The migration of social scientists from Third World countries to the developed countries does not appear to be a major problem generally though some countries such as Sri Lanka and India do seem to have lost some of their very distinguished social scientists in this manner.

2. Obstacles to the development of intra-regional and inter-regional co-operation among social scientists

(13) The similarities that exist between the different regions in respect of the state of social science have not yet given rise to intra-regional and inter-regional co-operation on a scale that might be considered adequate in the light of the desirability of and potential for such co-operation. The main obstacles that seem to hamper it are a nearly total absence of information; extremely inadequate documentation and communication services; insufficient personal contacts between social scientists; differing intellectual traditions which are a hangover from the days of colonial régimes; multiplicity of languages; long-standing relations between particular Third World countries and particular Western countries and the absence of any tradition of such contacts among the developing countries themselves.

(14) Two major factors limiting the growth of social sciences in the Third World countries which were particularly stressed were dearth of new information and inaccessibility of existing documentation. The latter is often located in the former imperial countries and efforts have to be made to either acquire them in original or to have them copied. These requisites along with others already mentioned (such as adequately trained personnel in sufficient numbers) constitute the infrastructure of social science research and this remains weak in all parts of the Third World, though perhaps less so in Latin America than in, say, Africa or Asia.

3. Promotion of social sciences and of co-operation among social scientists

(15) Given the circumstances, it is not surprising that a lot remains to be done to identify common urgent problems and to establish criteria of priority. In this connexion, there was general agreement that the responsibility for these tasks must be shouldered by the different countries themselves, acting individually or as collectivities at regional or inter-regional levels. Organizations like Unesco could only support social scientists and social science research institutions in their research endeavours; it could not identify for them what their research interests should be; it could only indicate what can be done. It was not for Unesco (and such other international organizations) to emphasize, play down or "invent" any problems but only to help in developing social sciences regionally and internationally. The challenges to social scientists should emanate from their immediate socio-cultural economic and political environments and they must develop adequate sensitivity to recognize and meet them. There is no substitute for self-awareness in this regard.

(16) In connexion with Unesco's rôle in promoting social sciences, it was also pointed out that an intervening factor was the government in each country though perhaps more so in some regions than in others. The policies of governments regarding social science research at home and collaboration in social science research on a regional basis would largely determine what the social scientists in each country can achieve. What is involved is not merely the science policy of a government but the nature of its domestic development programmes and its foreign policy. Some participants repeatedly pointed out that social scientists in some countries do not have adequate opportunities for meaningful work, are subject to various kinds of controls, and that social sciences have been in places and at times regarded as subversive. At the same time, it was pointed out that social scientists themselves often produced research results that were not usable by planners and managers.

(17) The meeting emphasized the rôle which national and international professional associations and councils can play in persuading individual social scientists to focus on socially relevant problems and in cultivating a regional perspective on the same. It was further suggested that national, intra-regional, inter-regional and international agencies ought to dovetail their activities in such a manner that the talents of social scientists are purposefully employed, evenly distributed, and adequately supported. Besides, all unnecessary wastage of resources, human and material, can be avoided by cross-country and inter-regional co-operation. The aim of co-operation between agencies operating at different levels should be to strengthen teaching and research programmes where they exist and to initiate them where they are absent.

(18) The meeting devoted considerable attention to the need for "indigenization". This was identified as a multi-dimensional endeavour which was already under way. In its most elementary form it consisted of the enlargement of national educational systems so that social science research in any particular country would be primarily in the hands of its nationals. Currently, it so happens, 90 per cent of all social scientists belong to the developed countries. This is obviously very unsatisfactory. Also, there is the increasing awareness that cultural, intellectual and financial dependence on outside agencies and institutions must end. There has long existed an imbalance between intellectual "imports" and "exports" between the Third World countries and the advanced nations of the West. There has been an abundant inflow into the developing countries of ready-made conceptual models, theoretical frameworks, research techniques, etc., whereas the flow in the reverse direction has been the raw data, whether collected by foreigners or "native" scholars. Also, by and large, formal classroom teaching has been the dominant if not exclusive

concern of social scientists in the Third World with the result that they have failed to conduct research extensively to come to grips with the real problems of development in their own countries.

(19) What is called for, therefore, is: re-definition of the goals of the educational systems; reformulation of curricula; reorganization of research to come to grips with nationally relevant issues and the demands of developmental efforts; recognition of alternatives to development as now defined; re-examination of the types of data to be collected and the manner of their collection; persuading governments to make greater use of social science expertise; etc. Indigenization means all these, but it does not mean shutting the social sciences up behind national curtains of various degrees of thickness and colour. It was emphasized that what the social scientists in the Third World are striving for is not the establishment of national modes of thinking or of different logics of social science. The aims and methods of social science are the same everywhere but the problems vary from country to country and region to region, entailing the fact that the application of social science research findings will be specific.

(20) Indigenization, by leading to a recognition of cultural specificities, has exposed the dangers of prevalent uni-factor theories of development, which have generally focused on the economic variable alone. A fragmentation of social science research which had thus resulted will be corrected by the shifting of emphasis from theoretical models of Western origin to multi-dimensional national problems and the task of solving them. Another danger to be avoided is that of an easy surrender to the pressing demands of governments for applied research within short periods of time. Such research is only as good as the foundations of sound theory and methodology on which it is built. The two types of research are mutually reinforcing and develop through a process of dialectical interaction. There is no real conflict between basic and applied research.

4. Co-operation within regions and between regions in the Third World and between the Third World and the developed countries

(21) Indigenization, it was agreed, was an essential condition for the further development of social sciences along socially meaningful lines in all regions of the world, but particularly in the so-called developing countries. It must mean self-reliance without parochialization. It follows, therefore, that hand in hand with the effort to relate social science effort in each country to the solution of its own specific practical problems and methodological concerns, deliberate action must be initiated to promote inter-country co-operation within each region and also inter-regional co-operation. Further, the existing "vertical" relationship between the social sciences in the Western

countries, particularly North America, and other parts of the world - a linkage which has sometimes been conceptualized as the "centre-periphery" relationship - must also be re-examined and redefined. This relationship had arisen owing to the fact that the intellectual "centres" from which the social scientists of these countries had drawn sustenance have been located in the West. The universities and research institutions of their own countries had constituted a kind of "periphery" of intellectual "outposts" in relation to these "centres". In the context of today's changed political situation, and widespread recognition of the importance of global co-operation it is apparent that this dependence has to end, and earlier imbalances have to be corrected. It was, however, pointed out that a somewhat altered international social stratification system exists today among social scientists as "centres" have emerged in some countries of the Third World itself. What we have today is a polycentric situation and co-operation among social scientists across countries and regions is often precluded by fears of intellectual (and perhaps even political) hegemony. Co-operation between social scientists among the developed and the developing nations has to be examined in the light of this complex situation.

(22) Certain basic queries were made in this connexion. Was the definition of regions implied by the manner in which background papers had been prepared for the meeting an acceptable one? If development is to be a principal focus for the future growth of social science effort, the relevance of political boundaries within which policies are made may not be doubted. But the compulsions of economic planning sometimes persuade even governments to look beyond their own territories. Should not, therefore, region be defined in ecological terms? Moreover, the present approach results in the juxtaposition of an internally well-knit region such as the Arab region, or a relatively small region such as the European region, alongside of the very large, internally diverse region of Asia. It would be much more meaningful to think of Asia in terms of sub-regions. But the splitting of Africa below and above the Sahara also is problematic. Besides the difficulties attending upon the use of the word region, even the notion of the Third World creates problems, resulting from the cross-cutting of economic and cultural conditions. Thus where does Japan belong? Internal diversities in levels of overall development, which encompass the development of social sciences also, in all regions but especially in some, make the task of inter-regional co-operation both important and at the same time difficult. There lurks in the shadows the possibility of the emergence of vertical relations within the regions. Finally, there are practical problems to be overcome before co-operative research efforts can materialize. Governments will have to be persuaded about the utility of such joint endeavours; linguistic barriers

will have to be overcome; resistances emanating from the different modes of the organization of scientific communities (their peculiar social stratification systems) will also have to be overcome; the comparability of data will have to be assured; so on and so forth. The first conclusion that seems to emerge in this context is the significantly important rôle which international organizations such as Unesco can play to smooth and strengthen co-operation. It has been the experience of most social scientists that cross-country comparative research projects are generally more acceptable if they are carried out under the auspices of some international organization, if they focus on the problems of the developing countries, and if they do not preempt the right of the social scientists of these countries to determine priorities and choose research themes.

(23) The need for the clarification of general issues does not, however, constitute an argument against the very basic need for intra-regional and inter-regional co-operation. The economic advantages of pooled efforts (for instance, in the shape of data banks and computer facilities) between neighbouring countries within regions are obvious. The duplication of such efforts in different parts of Europe is a wastage of resources which the developing countries must avoid. Besides the consideration of economies, there is also the intellectual fascination and importance of comparative studies which underlines the importance of co-operation between countries. Many problems, such as the population explosion, many concerns such as the preservation of the environment, and many programmes such as the introduction of new technologies in agriculture are common to all regions, and it would be not only sensible but indeed essential to pool efforts in these fields.

(24) The mechanisms of achieving such co-operation are another matter, however, and need to be carefully attended to. Joint research endeavours can be undertaken under the auspices of governmental or autonomous agencies, regional or sub-regional professional associations, and international organizations. What is needed is the compilation of information about such agencies where it is not already available.

5. Recommendations for intra-regional and inter-regional co-operation

(25) Throughout the deliberations, especially in discussing common problems relating to the development of social science, suggestions were put forward for action to be undertaken in order to improve the situation. It was the opinion of the meeting that, by and large, the problems of intra-regional and inter-regional co-operation were similar, though the agencies responsible for bringing it about were not the same at the two levels involved.

(26) Europe and North America as developed regions bear special responsibilities for enhancing inter-regional co-operation. As noted earlier in this report, traditional patterns of academic collaboration between the developed and developing countries have tended to reinforce this dominance of the former over the latter due to a sheer imbalance in social science resources. Genuine partnership should, on the other hand, aim at helping develop "endogenous" social sciences responsive to the values and needs of a given country or region. The meeting recognized rich potentials of the social sciences in Europe and North America which have to be fully utilized in strengthening co-operation internationally. With this fundamental principle and regional variations in mind, the concerned organizations - national, regional, inter-regional and international - are invited to undertake suitable action along the following lines:

(i)   Generation, accumulation, storage, dissemination and protection of research information and data relevant to the analysis of local social situations. This would include basic information regarding who is doing what, where, how and why?

(ii)   Exchange of research instruments (i.e. research designs, questionnaires, interview schedules) and reports.

(iii)   Exchange of scholars at different levels within and between regions.

(iv)   Provision for training at leading educational and research institutions within a region and the development there of relevant curricula, research techniques, etc., keeping in mind common regional developmental needs.

(v)   Preparation and publication of relevant textbooks and source books within the region.

(vi)   Publication of directories of ongoing research and of research results in scholarly publications including regional bulletins and journals (e.g. Journal of Asian/African/Latin American Studies).

(vii)   Provision of facilities for language teaching and for translation from one language of a region to another.

(viii) Establishment of regional and sub-regional documentation centres, data banks, computer centres, etc., for which the Vienna Centre's experience might be valuable.

(ix)   Initiation of regional and inter-regional cross-country comparative research studies, particularly on developmental problems (see paragraph 26).

(x)   Organization of study groups, workshops, training programmes, seminars, etc., to develop technical expertise in the social sciences and make it more widely available on a regional and inter-regional basis with a view to ending the dependence of the developing countries on the advanced countries. Such meetings could also discuss particular research projects with a view to clarifying objectives and devising appropriate techniques.

(xi) Institutionalization of inter-regional contacts through, for instance, general assemblies of regional organizations, to be attended by, among others, their chief executives. Also arrangements should be made to enable representatives of regional organizations to attend one another's executive committee meetings. Finally, there should be provision for inter-regional meetings for the discussion of social science development under the auspices of international organizations, notably Unesco.

(27) As regards research themes suitable for comparative study, the meeting made the following general recommendations, leaving it to the participants and other social scientists to evolve specific proposals on their basis:

(i)   Alternative models of development.
(ii)   Social problems arising out of development.
(iii) Preservation of environment and natural resources.
(iv)   Transformation of agrarian structure.
(v)   Development of modern occupations and professions.

(vi)   Transfer of technology.
(vii) Evaluation of foreign aid.
(viii) Rôle of multinationals.
(ix)   Contribution of social sciences to development.
(x)   The new socio-economic order.

(28) Apropos the suggestions contained in the foregoing paragraphs, two major caveats were entered: (i) it was emphasized that co-operation is not to be considered an unquestioned value in itself, desirable in all forms at all times and in all places. It was pointed out that co-operative research need not and should not be allowed to militate against the fundamental aim of developing social sciences as well and as fully as desirable at the national level. The success of regional and inter-regional co-operative research will ultimately depend upon national efforts in the development of social sciences; (ii) it was noted that research efforts of the kind proposed at the meeting raised basic questions about the nature of social science and about techniques of comparison which also must engage the attention of social scientists all over the world.

CHAPTER 2

Social Science Co-operation in Asia
by
Ramashray Roy
Former Secretary-General of the
Association of Asian Social Science Research Councils

I. THE PROBLEM

The countries of what is non-stigmatically called
the developing world are engaged in the stupendous
task of modernizing their societies. The process
of induced modernization is bringing about changes -
slow, uneven and imperceptible in many cases, to
be sure - in the social, economic and political
structures in these countries. These changes as
well as the difficulty in quickening the pace of
change have progressively created two types of
awareness. In the first place, it is now increasingly felt that the capacity of a particular country
to succeed in its drive towards modernity is dependent upon forces not under its control. In the
second place, it is also appreciated that modernization cannot be conceived simply in terms of economic growth since cultural and social factors impinge heavily on developmental process. The
former emphasizes the existence of certain impediments that cannot be successfully tackled by a single
country and therefore must be handled on the basis
of co-operation among several countries. The latter, in turn, underlines the inadequacy of economic
approach to modernization and highlights the necessity of calling upon the social sciences to co-operate
in the endeavour of national transformation which
has so far been the preserve of economics alone.

The realization of the necessity of launching co-
operative effort involving several countries for
solving problems that a single nation finds it difficult to handle has, during the recent years, led to
the establishment of various regional organizations.
These organizations provide structural framework
for identifying and defining problems requiring co-
ordinated efforts of several countries, mobilization
of resources for coping with the problems they encounter, and allocating responsibilities of implementation. Thus, there has decisively occurred a
shift away from a rigid conception of sovereignty
towards interdependence at least in so far as the
solution of problems in economic and related fields
is concerned.

While interdependence in the economic field is

an established fact, this is not the case in so far
as inter-regional co-operation in the social sciences in Asia is concerned. It is not that efforts
towards promoting such a co-operation is lacking.
As a matter of fact, Unesco and other international
agencies have been active in this area for a long
time now. However, the inward orientation of social scientists in various countries of Asia remains
a dominant tendency even today. It should be pointed
out that the first serious effort to build bridges between Asian countries was made by Unesco in the
year 1954, when a Round-Table Conference was
convened on the Teaching of the Social Sciences in
South Asia ... in Delhi from 15 to 19 February
1954. The Round-Table Conference came out with
a series of recommendations and underlined the
whole question of communication, interchange,
and assimilation as between East and West, including certain aspects of the problems of language as
a tool of science.

One of the important suggestions made at the
Round Table concerned the necessity of maintaining
regular contacts between the scholars of the Asian
countries. As Atal points out, "These pious hopes
and recommendations never got implemented, however, geographically proximate social scientists
of the region still remain academically remote.
They share a common cultural heritage of the East
but do not have a co-operative fund of contemporary
knowledge"(1).

This persistence of the trend of isolationism
requires explanation. The purpose of this paper
is to focus on the weakness of inter-regional co-
operation in the social sciences in Asia. Towards
this end, we, first, examine the specific characteristics of social science research in Asia. We
will be particularly concerned in this connexion with
the issue of indigenization versus universalization
of social sciences. We then discuss possibilities
of co-operation between the developing regions,
on the one hand, and between the developing and

(1) Yogesh Atal, ed. , Social Sciences in Asia,
New Delhi, Abhinav Publications, 1974, 12 p.

the developed nations, on the other. We discuss next some of the existing mechanisms of regional social science co-operation in Asia. Lastly, we suggest some steps that should be taken to facilitate inter-regional co-operation in the social sciences.

II. FACTORS IMPEDING SOCIAL SCIENCE GROWTH IN ASIA

Impediments to growth of inter-regional co-operative effort in the realm of social sciences in Asia are numerous. However, for the purposes of this paper, we can identify three major factors that have impinged heavily on not only the pattern of growth of social sciences in different countries of Asia but also on the prospects of co-operation in the social sciences transcending national boundaries in the Asian region. These factors are: historical experience, the transnational system of social sciences, and the pressure of national development. Historically speaking, most of the Asian countries have for long been protected from the cataclysmic changes brought about by industrialization and other related processes. As a result, these societies have been quiescent- even though politically turbulent at times. And quiescent societies do not enrich social sciences. Social sciences in Asia have largely been implanted by the countries of the West and have grown in a transnational system of asymmetry and dependence. More recently, the stupendous task of nation-building undertaken by all countries of Asia has created a situation where social science expertise and energy must be devoted to the immediate problem of smoothing the course of social and economic development.

1. Historical experience

Referring to the birth of sociology, Durkheim remarks that sociology could have been born and developed where two conditions existed in combination. First, traditionalism had to have lost its domain. Among a people who consider their institutions everything they ought to be, nothing can incite thought to apply itself to social matters. Second, a veritable faith in the power of reason to dare to undertake the translation of the most complex and unstable of realities into definite terms was necessary[1]. These two conditions were present in the West at the onset of industrial revolution and the new science of society emerged both as a response to problems that became manifest in times of rapid social change and as a dissatisfaction with the inadequacies of the then existing disciplines - philosophy, political economy and law - in encompassing the range of social phenomena encountered in the real world.

The twin conditions - that is, disintegration of traditionalism and faith in the power of science

to examine social realities with a view to remaking reality rather than merely adjusting to it - were lacking in the countries of Asia. The social order was taken for granted as well as felt to be satisfying. The stability of social forms, despite occasional political turbulences, did everything to deaden the sense of the problematic. Since men cherished the values, the norms and social forms inherited from their ancestors and since nothing was problematic, there was no occasion to apply reason to remaking reality.

However, confrontation with the West initiated dramatic changes in these societies. One of the most far-reaching implications of this confrontation was the creation of the awareness of alternative structures of social order. The awareness of the existence of other ways of seeing the world, in turn, produces a situation of choice and an inclination to apply reason to overcome anomalies characterizing the obtaining social reality. In other words, it is the development of self-awareness that gives birth to the new science of society. The confrontation with the West did create a sense of awareness in the minds of intelligentsia in the Asian countries; however, such an awareness was largely the product of Western thought-ways. As Pieris observes, "But since the changes which took place in colonial times were exogenous, triggered by alien domination, a good deal of social thought was implanted, and drew the attention of the colonial intelligentsia to the features of Western industrial society"[2].

The shaping of the self-awareness of the intelligentsia in the Asian countries took place in the seats of higher learning modelled upon those in the West. Whether the initiative in introducing modern education was taken by colonial rulers or indigenous régimes, the fact remains that the development of social sciences in Asian countries has been closely bound up with the pragmatic considerations of the rulers. As Chomchai observes in the case of Thailand, "Even before the first university was founded just before the end of the First World War, the demands of government have dictated the organization of instruction in the social sciences, though only a restricted group of people had direct access to it".[3] What is true of Thailand is also true of other countries in Asia. In India, for example, the introduction of modern education under the British rule was with a view

(1) E. Durkheim, "Sociology" (translated by J. D. Folkman) in K. Wolff (ed.), Emile Durkheim, 1858-1917; Columbus, Ohio State University Press, 1960, 383 p.
(2) Ralph Pieris, "The Implantation of Sociology in Asia", International Social Science Journal (Paris), Vol. XXI, No. 3, 1969, p. 435.
(3) Prachoom Chomchai, "Implantation and Acclimatization of the Social Sciences in Thailand", International Social Science Journal (Paris), Vol. XXI, No. 3, 1969, p. 384.

primarily to training professionals capable of assisting in the task of governance.

It is out of this pragmatic consideration that the various disciplines of social sciences developed. However, they were implanted on the Asian soil without due regard for the different social conditions prevailing in different countries. Based on and incorporating Western experience and thought-ways, the implanted social sciences could never relate themselves to their immediate environment and its characteristics and therefore failed in promoting an awareness among the colonial intelligentsia of examining concrete reality in their own homelands for remaking their own societies. To quote Pieris again:

"But rather than adopt aims and methods that since the Renaissance proved fruitful for the study of Western society, that is, through humanistic scholarship, colonial savants outside the political arcana adopted the intellectual heritage of conquest without demur. It is significant that the most dehumanized forms of sociology and economics gained currency in colonial universities, although they had no relevance for the study of Asian conditions, and this intellectual dependence continued in the two decades after independence. Indigenous scholars hugged these intellectual chains because they thought they were accepting aims and methods of universal validity"(1).

Apart from this intellectual dependence, the development of social sciences in many of the Asian countries is very recent(2) and characterized by a tension of contrary pulls of competing approaches. Broadly speaking, two patterns of development of social science disciplines in the Asian countries are discernible. First, in many of the universities social sciences have developed piecemeal. That is to say, a "core" discipline was introduced first around which other disciplines were built gradually and installed as separate departments at a later time. Second, in some of the universities, mostly the newly established ones, the whole gamut of social science disciplines was introduced all at once.

However, what is noteworthy with either pattern is, one, the rigidities of disciplinary boundaries and, two, too much strong emphasis on formal teaching to the detriment of research and development. The inability of the departmental structures of the universities has, in several cases, led to the establishment of research institutions outside the university structure. However, the lack of communication between university departments and research institutions prevents the incorporation of research findings in social science syllabi. As a result, a duality exists which means that while the new research institutions have based their researches and theories and methodologies developed in recent years, the teaching of social sciences proceeds on the traditional lines. This duality is all the more accentuated since universities, in

general, impart a routinized science which requires no original research or creative thinking.

The historical experience of almost all the Asian countries in terms of the development of social sciences highlights the exogenous origin of social sciences. This has shaped intellectual perspectives of the intelligentsia in the Asia countries oriented largely towards and pulled by some central gravity in the West. The lack of appreciation of scientific values in the indigenous culture reinforced this tendency. The rigidity of the departmental structure in the universities, disciplinary parochialism, and archaic course contents hampered the promotion of social science research in the universities. The establishment of research centres outside the university structure brought into being a duality which precluded meaningful communication and interaction between teaching and research. Furthermore, the shortage of trained manpower also meant deflection of social science personnel to pursuits other than teaching and research.

2.   The transnational system of social sciences

The period after the Second World War is interesting for the development of social science in Asia for various reasons. First, many of the Asian countries attained freedom from alien rule and found themselves occupying crucial positions in world politics and discharging important rôles in various world organizations. The shift of dominant centres of social science from Europe to the United States and her expanded rôle in the international arena suddenly promoted a great interest in comparative studies and launched, as a result, large scale collaborative research programmes involving several countries in the developed and the developing regions. This meant, in effect, a new rôle for social scientists in the developing countries since they were now called upon to participate in international research projects in addition to their other responsibilities, such as teaching.

Second, the necessity of speeding up the process of economic and social change in the developing countries further involved social scientists in research in order to clarify policy choices, analyse difficulties in implementation and evaluate performance. The demand on social scientists to contribute to the developmental effort of the country has been increasing as the realization of the non-technical factors impinging on social development has sharpened in the developing countries. Since the countries of the Third World are passing through the crisis of change, social scientists are asked not only to account for and explain it, but also to deal with it.

(1) Ralph Pieris, op. cit., p. 438.
(2) See, for example, various country papers in Yogesh Atal (ed.), op. cit.

Thus both external and internal environments began, in the post Second World War period, making claims on the expertise of social scientists in the developing countries. However, the structure of the transnational system of social science was highly asymmetrical and therefore led to dependency relations between social scientists in the developing countries and those in the developed countries[1]. Several factors combined to produce this dependency relationship. First, dominant theories and methodologies in the developed countries served as world-wide guide-posts for both teaching and research. Before World War II, Europe provided the frame of reference for teaching and research in the Asian countries. This changed after the Second World War and the United States emerged as the dominant centre radiating critical impulses for orienting teaching and research in the developing countries. This continues even now. Moreover, the developed countries still provide the training ground for social scientists in the developing countries. However, such a training emphasizes techniques, values and problems that are more relevant to conditions in the developed countries than in the developing countries.

Second, asymmetry in the transnational social science system and the consequent dependence relationship is, in a sense, the outgrowth of the more profound economic and political inequalities characterizing the world community. The initial difference in the level of economic development is reflected in the level of development of social sciences also. This difference is reflected in access to greater resource base in the developed countries. Note, for example, the facts that greater resources are available in the developed countries for advancing social science knowledge; there is greater concentration in the developed countries of means of publishing and distributing research findings; and the major academic centres are located in the developing countries. In contrast, lacking in resources, the developing countries are not in a position to create necessary infrastructures for the support and growth of social sciences. Most importantly there is also the fact of the very small size of the social science community in each of the developing countries which is under pressure not only to make its contribution to the growth of social sciences but also to undertake administrative and political responsibilities which naturally reduce the time and resources it can devote to advanced research and training[2].

The cumulative impact of the asymmetric nature of the transnational system of social sciences and the consequent dependence relation is reflected in two crucial ways. First, the gross inequality in the distribution of resources for teaching and research in itself constitutes a severe restraint on the growth process of social sciences in the developing countries. A large part of resources available for research and development in the developing countries is channelled to natural sciences and related activities. While the awareness of the potential contribution of social sciences to national developmental effort is growing, the imbalance in resource allocation still persists. As a result, we witness in the developing countries the phenomenon of what is commonly called "the brain drain", on the one hand, and the persisting lack of basic facilities for undertaking fundamental research in theory and methodology, on the other.

Second, the continuance of the dominance of theories and methodologies derived from the experiences of the industrialized countries still remains a major characteristic of the transnational social science system. Derived from the cultural tradition and historical experiences of the West, these theories and methodologies are ill-suited to conditions prevailing in the developed

---

(1) For an extended discussion on this aspect, see Chadwick Alger and Gene M. Lyons, "Social Science as a Transnational System", _International Social Science Journal_ (Paris), Vol. XXVI, No. 1, 1974, pp. 137-149. This is a report of a seminar on "Social Sciences as a Transnational System", held in Bellagio, Italy, from 16 to 21 July 1973.

(2) There are exceptions, though. However, asymmetric relations are also reflected internally in the developing countries. This works in two ways. First, there is a great disparity in the resource allocation to scientific and to social science research and development. As Adiseshiah points out in relation to the situation in India, "The present position is that the country is spending annually about Rs. 2,500 million on research and development in the natural, technological, agricultural and medical sciences and around Rs. 25 million on research in social sciences. This, I believe, is a serious imbalance". M. A. Adiseshiah, Presidential Address to Asian Conference on Teaching and Research in Social Sciences, in Yogesh Atal, ed., op. cit., p. 47.

Second, there is a pronounced tendency among those who participate in transnational activities to constitute an élite group. This makes it possible for them to have greater access to resources and opportunities than other social scientists. It should also be pointed out that these élites usually have interests and perspectives which are not usually shared by their colleagues and compatriots. In such a situation, a large part of research opportunities are utilized by these élites and this brings into being a dependence relationship between them and their colleagues.

countries(1) since they represent altogether different stages of social and economic development. Influenced by these theories and methodologies, social scientists in the developing countries tend to look at the problems in their own country through a prismatic glass which assumes different colours in response to light transmitted from the developed world. The dominant theories and methodologies become, as Alger and Lyons observe, "instruments not only of scientific advancement, but also of political power that tends to perpetuate the existing structure of international relations"(2).

3.   The pressure of national development

Apart from the relative weakness of the social sciences in the developing countries and their dependence for teaching and research on dominant imported theories and methodologies, the pressure of national development itself acts as a constraint on the growth of and inter-regional co-operation in the social sciences in certain situations. It does not need to be demonstrated that the pressure of development felt in all the developing countries acts to orient teaching and research to problems that are encountered in the process of social change. Denigrated in this process are all efforts towards theory-building and innovation in methodology and, as a consequence, allocation of resources to such activities is decried as wasteful. This naturally puts accentuated emphasis on "applied" research as against "fundamental" research. This is illustrated by the establishment of a Ministry for National Research in Indonesia and its announced policy that "the task of research workers should be to undertake investigation within the framework of the National Development Plan"(3).

As the Review Committee of the Indian Council of Social Science Research observes in the case of India:

"Much of the current research effort has no relevance to contemporary social and national problems and suffers besides from lack of rigour in its analysis of phenomena and synthesis of facts. It is largely oriented to micro-level research to the neglect of macro-level problems. It is not yet emancipated from its tutelage to Western theories and has failed to develop research tools, designs, and models of its own, appropriate to the Indian situation"(4).

It further says that, "Today India needs social science research which is significant and at the same time relevant to its national goals and objectives, as ICSSR is a public agency which draws its resources entirely from public funds"(5).

This emphasis on "relevant" research - relevant in the sense of helping the developmental process of the country - affects, on the one hand, the growth of social sciences themselves and, on the other, the possibilities of inter-regional co-operation in the social sciences. The call for a

greater emphasis on "applied" social science, no doubt, derived from the urgency of seeking solutions to manifold pressing problems. However, such a call assumes that the theories and methodologies included in the repertoire of a social scientist are capable enough to provide answers to urgent questions. As a matter of fact, two factors combine to make much of social science knowledge difficult to apply to concrete situations. First, since the dominant theories and methodologies are derived from the cultural tradition and historical experiences of the industrialized societies, they are not helpful in making appraisal of and suggesting remedies for continuing anomalies in the developing countries.

Second, the thrust of empiricism in social science research with its emphasis on the construction of a grand theory restricts the choice of research strategy as well as explanatory framework for understanding social reality.

As Silvert argues:

"The common denominator of all these constructions is that they attempt a total explanation from an intellectual base somewhere outside of man's historical experience. Now I see nothing objectionable in aspiring to a universal theory of social action, but to argue that there is master principle, or even a set of principles, to which societies conform is not the way to achieve it ... (T)hese approaches do not provide sufficient conditions for explaining any particular cases. Further, the ideological effect of such views is to persuade us that the ways in which man can make his world are depressingly limited"(6).

The denigration of general theory is based on the fact that a general theory fails to take into account the variability of human situation and experience. Research based on such a perspective is thus incapacitated from providing relevant answers

(1)   It should be pointed out here that these theories and methodologies are by no means monolithic, they range from Marxist to non-Marxist to anti-Marxist theories and methodologies. However, the fact remains that they are rooted in Western experience and as perspectives on social reality, they retain their alienness in the context of the developing countries.
(2)   Alger and Lyons, op. cit., p. 139.
(3)   Unesco Research Centre on Social and Economic Development in Southern Asia, Delhi, "Social Science Research in Indonesia", Internal Paper No. 1, 1965 (Mimeo), p. 4.
(4)   Indian Council of Social Science Research, Review Committee, A Report on Social Sciences in India: Retrospective and Perspective, p. 62, ICSSR, New Delhi, 1973, Vol. 1.
(5)   Ibid., p. 123.
(6)   Kalman H. Silvert, Man's Power: Biased Guide to Political Thought and Action, pp. 8-9, New York, The Viking Press, 1970.

for solving concrete problems. Furthermore, it should also be recognized that there is a very limited range of problems on which truly applied research can be fruitfully conducted. Applied research can succeed only in cases where the range of variables is very small, the sequence of causal linkage very short, and the interplay of conflicting values non-existent. However, social problems are not so simple. Here multiple variables in their multivariability are involved, the chain of reciprocal influence pattern is very complex and long and conflict of values overly accentuated. To call for increased applied research in the murky area of social relations with unfinished and largely unfashioned tools of social science theory is to overstate the capacity of applied research.

And yet the insistence on applied social science research is a fact in the developing countries. To the extent that such an insistence gets reflected in decisions with respect to setting priorities in social science research and allocating research, the need for fashioning new theories and forging useful methodologies relevant to the experience of the developing countries goes by default. And without investing requisite resources in the development of relevant theories and methodologies, the basis of applied research itself would remain weak. Thus, the pressure of national development acts as a deterrent to the growth of social sciences in the developing countries.

The pressure of national development acts also to discourage inter-regional co-operation in the social sciences. Since the accent is placed heavily on solving problems that are encountered within the framework of the national society and since configuration of these problems differs from one country to the next, it is natural for social scientists to devote their energies to studying national problems. This tendency is further reinforced by the fact that the size of well-trained social scientists is very small in the developing countries.

Our argument thus far highlights three factors that impinge upon the possibility of inter-regional co-operation in the social sciences in Asia. The first factor concerns the historical experience with respect to social sciences in Asian countries. Social sciences, like other sciences, are implanted in Asia. As such, they reflect a perspective that developed out of cultural tradition and historical experiences of Western countries. Their "alienness" in the Asian countries is matched by the lack of a wider support in the populace in so far as it manifests cultural values, beliefs and attitudes discounting human intervention for remaking society. In addition to the recency and the haphazard growth of social sciences in Asia, there is also the factor of lower priority and smaller resources allocated to the growth of social sciences. Starting from this comparatively weak position, social scientists in the Asian countries have had to face the asymmetric nature of the transnational system of

social sciences which reinforced their dependency on the developed countries. Equally important in this regard is the pressure to orient social science teaching and research to developmental needs of the Asian countries which, again, impinges very substantially on the growth of social sciences.

These factors have combined to prevent the emergence of truly inter-regional co-operation in the social sciences in Asia. Since most of the Asian countries have lacked resources for supporting large-scale social science research, many of the social scientists have been attracted to participate in research activities undertaken by academic centres in the developed countries. Thus "Asian scholars were devoting themselves to problems and areas of research determined in the West, using Western methods and theories"(1). The extent of dependency can be gauged by the fact that many social scientists in the developing countries have had to participate in research which they do not consider as a priority problem but which is given emphasis by those who control research support from abroad. It is, however, the élite among the social scientists that is co-opted in the transnational system of the social sciences. A large number of "non-élite" social scientists have of necessity to engage in micro-studies since their access to resources is very meagre. The proliferation of micro-studies is a fact in the Asian countries. A heavy reliance on such studies has precluded a macro-social perspective which is essential for understanding the enlarged networks of relationships that affect smaller units. It also precluded the emergence of a comparative method vital for understanding macro-social complexes. But "this was ruled out because colonial rule had created a number of non-communicating 'corridors' which linked the intelligentsia of each colony to some distant intellectual centre of gravity in the Occident. Their 'underdeveloped' neighbours were of no interest"(2).

If the dependency relationship established communicating doors between the developed and developing countries, the pressure for harnessing social science teaching and research to serving national developmental purposes has acted to orient and channel social science energy inward. Both these developments affect adversely the prospect of inter-regional co-operation in the social sciences in Asia.

Recent years have, however, witnessed a qualitative change in the atmosphere. Dissatisfaction with imported theories and methodologies has been mounting. While it is in part a mirror effect of a similar dissatisfaction with dependence relations in economic and political realms, it is also in part due to a growing awareness of the gross limitations of the dominant paradigms of social science research and their unsuitability to

(1) Ralph Pieri, op. cit., p. 441.
(2) Ralph Pieri, op. cit., p. 437

conditions obtaining in the developing parts of the world. It is not surprising, therefore, to encounter the escalating demand in the developing countries for "relevant", "useful", "applied" social science research and teaching. Obviously, the emphasis here is on developing theories and methodologies based on and catering to the needs of national experience and purpose. As Kothari puts it, "India will never be truly free until its intellectuals and social scientists think for themselves and develop their own paradigms based on their own values and cultural orientations"[1]. It is this turning away that is creating an interest in developing neighbours and opening up new corridors of communication among the developing countries and promoting the erection of structures for facilitating inter-regional co-operation in the social sciences in Asia.

This, however, raises two questions. First, what implications does this turning away have for the universality of social science knowledge? This turning away has been variously described as "indigenization", "regionalization", etc., of social sciences and it is feared that this trend may result in a split or automization of the social sciences into different mutually incompatible schools. How far is this misgiving true? Or, to take another tack, what is the meaning of "indigenization" and to what extent is it reflected in the research efforts of the developing countries? Second, given the growing awareness of the need for co-operative efforts transcending national boundaries, how can such a co-operation be strengthened between developing countries, on the one hand, and between developing and developed countries, on the other? It is to a discussion of these two questions that now we turn.

III. TRENDS TOWARDS INDIGENIZATION AND REGIONALIZATION

The phenomenon of self-awareness among social scientists in the Asian countries is very recent. It is the product of their experiences with the transnational system of social sciences, on the one hand, and the internal pressure for playing a more useful rôle in nation-building efforts. This self-awareness manifests itself in various ways: tendency to reject theories and methodologies originating in the West, the felt need to derive them on the basis of the unique historical experiences of the countries of Asia, and greater awareness of an interest in other developing countries at a similar stage of development. The growing dissatisfaction with Western dominance in the realm of social sciences has provoked the phenomenon of self-assertion on the part of Asian social scientists.

This self-assertion is taking two forms at the present. In the first place, a tendency towards "indigenization" of social science is gathering strength. This tendency is reflected in such efforts

as developing social-science paradigms on the basis of indigenous values and cultural orientations, articulating social science research questions in the context of national developmental needs and aspirations, and setting up of social science councils or some similar bodies in different Asian countries to formulate research priorities and fund research projects. In the second place, the turning away from the developed countries has also meant an appreciation of similar destiny of the developing countries and a growing realization of the necessity to know each other better and, therefore, of forging co-operative relationships for promoting social sciences. This trend can be called regionalization of social sciences.

In this context two points need to be dwelt upon here. The first concerns the recent efforts towards developing co-operative relationships and devising institutional structures to sustain these relationships. The second point concerns the effect of indigenization and regionalization on the universality of social science knowledge. To begin with the first point, it should be emphasized here that previously social scientists from developing countries would usually meet with one another and collaborate in some research venture only through the dispensation of some academic centre in the developed world or through some international agency. This situation has, however, changed. The need for a mediator to arrange meetings between social scientists from the developing countries is swiftly giving way to direct contacts. With the formation of social science research councils or similar bodies in more and more Asian countries, establishing and maintaining of direct contact has become easier and institutionalized[2].

The growing awareness of co-operation has led to the formation of a few Asia-wide organizations and the organization of conferences and seminars for discussing ways and means of promoting co-operation in social science research and training. For example, the Asian Association of Development Research and Training Institutes was established in 1971 with its Headquarters in Bangkok. The main objective of this Association is to promote research and training activities in

(1) Rajni Kothari, Abstracts of the paper entitled "Values and Paradigms in Indian Social Science", submitted to the 29th International Congress of Orientalists, Paris, 16-22 July 1973.
(2) It is worth while to mention some of these agencies. These are: National Science Development Board, Philippines, established in 1958 with a Division of Social Sciences, Humanities and Statistics; National Research Council, Thailand, established in 1959; Indonesian Institute of Sciences, Indonesia, established in 1969; Indian Council of Social Science Research established in 1969.

Asia through closer co-operation between institutes in the field of economic and social development. It has organized five co-operative research groups in the areas of (a) plan implementation; (b) green revolution; (c) employment and unemployment; (d) growth of GNP and growth of income inequalities; and (e) urbanization. Its main functions are: (a) exchange of information relating to research and training activities; (b) promoting English translation of important publications and documents in indigenous languages; (c) promoting collaboration in research and training activities; (d) assisting in the development of particular research and· training programmes in institutes of the region and helping to secure the necessary assistance from within and without the region; (e) organization of working groups, seminars and conferences; and (f) issue of publications relevant to the activities of the Association[1].

Another important step in this direction was the convening of the Asian Conference of Teaching and Research in Social Sciences in Simla, India in May 1973[2]. Referring to the need for continuous association and interaction among social science researchers in Asia the Conference set up an association of Asian Social Science Research Councils (AASSREC). The functions of the Association were defined as (1) exchange of information among Asian social scientists; (2) exchange of scholars; (3) promotion of research opportunities for junior social scientists; (4) promotion of joint research programmes. The Conference also recommended that National Social Science Research Councils, should be expeditiously established in all those Asian countries where such a council, or its equivalent, does not exist. In addition, the Conference took this opportunity to impress upon Unesco for providing assistance and co-operation in the setting up of National Social Science Research Councils, reflecting of major Asian concerns in its programme, organizing a massive programme for institutional development for social sciences in Asia including the establishment of an Asian Institute of Social Sciences providing adequate representation of Asian social scientists in its department of social sciences[3].

The growing awareness of the need for co-operation also manifests itself in regional symposia and conferences. A particular mention may be made of the Symposium on Sociology and Social Development in Asia held in October 1973 in Tokyo. Following the deliberations, the symposium discussed the rôle of sociologists in social development and regional co-operation of sociologists in Asia[4]. The most recent example is that of the International Seminar on Inter-regional Co-operation in South and South East Asia held in Hyderabad (India) from 2 to 5 January 1975. Following discussions on (a) process of planning and plan implementation; (b) process of urbanization and problems of urbanization; (c) problems of bureaucracy and political development; and (d) problems

of plural societies; the seminar requested the members to initiate action with a view to undertaking cross-country research through universities and research institutions by entering into bilateral and multilateral agreements with one another.

These developments indicate at once a dual trend towards "indigenization" as well as "regionalization" of social sciences in Asia. Both of these tendencies, as we have pointed out, have their genesis in a sharp reaction against the dominance of Western theories and methodologies - a dominance reinforced by a greater concentration of resources in the developed part of the world. These tendencies, it should also be emphasized, are not antithetical. The universality assumption behind these theories, it is felt, does injustice to empirical conditions obtaining in the Asian countries. A strong emphasis is placed in different countries of Asia on building up their own social sciences "capable of providing a set of concepts and theories that will permit more adequate description of their societies than do the concepts and theories developed in Europe and America[5]. This is obviously an attempt to indigenize social sciences. However, such an attempt also brings into sharp focus the similarity of situations obtaining in most of the Asian countries, on the one hand, and the desirability of understanding larger societal processes that influence micro-level social interactions emphasizing the need of evolving cross-cultural comparative perspective on the other. Thus "indigenization" is a necessary step towards putting social sciences in a larger frame of reference provided by inter-regional co-operation.

This, however, raises the question of potential tension between "indigenization" and "universalization" of social sciences. At one level, the imposition of dichotomy between indigenization and universalization of social sciences is false on two counts. First, this dichotomy is perceived in the

(1) Development Centre of the Organization for Economic Co-operation and Development, Liaison Bulletin (Paris), No.2 (1972), pp.185-186
(2) Representatives of Afghanistan, Bangladesh, Cambodia, India, Indonesia, Iran, Japan, Laos, Nepal, Philippines, Singapore, South Korea, Sri Lanka and Thailand participated in the Conference.
(3) D. R. Rajalingam, "Rapporteur General's Report", in Atal, op. cit. , pp. 56-61.
(4) "Regionalization of Social Sciences in Latin America, Asia and Africa", International Social Science Journal (Paris), Vol. XXV, No. 4 (1973), p. 559.
(5) J. Szozepanski, "The International Sociological Association and Development of World Sociology", Sociological Abstracts, Vol. 16, No. 1, 15 February 1968. Szozepanski refers here to sociology but it is true as well of other social science disciplines.

context of national social science communities, especially in the developing regions, articulating national orientations in social science research and training. It is felt that such a national orientation is likely to deny the universality of social science knowledge.

It is not clear what precisely does the term "universality" mean in this connexion. It is sometimes used to mean the indivisibility of social science knowledge. In this sense it refers to a common stock of knowledge, access to which is free for all nations and to which they contribute according to their capacity. In another sense, by universality is meant that concepts and theories of social sciences are universally applicable irrespective of differences in historical experiences and socio-economic development of different nations.

In yet another sense, it is equated with internationalism and a distinction is made between internationality of science standing in striking contrast to the inevitable nationality of scientists[1]. In this sense, it refers largely to diffusion of knowledge and co-operation among social scientists across national boundaries. Deriving the "innately non-national character of science" from the unitary nature of physical reality, Storer does recognize the understanding of the unitary nature to be universal but goes on to suggest that "the existence of national boundaries should be completely irrelevant to (social scientists') concern for each other's work and their natural tendency to co-operate (even if antagonistically) in advancing the scientific understanding of this phenomenon"[2].

There is no ground to see any antagonism between "universalism" and "indigenization" or "regionalization" if universalism of social sciences is taken in the first sense. But trouble starts when it is assumed that the prevalent dominant concepts and theories have universal validity. As has been indicated earlier, the prevalent dominant concepts and theories are rooted in the cultural tradition and historical experience of the industrialized countries of the West. It is precisely this nature of the dominant concepts and theories that make them unsuitable for most of the developing countries. It is also precisely this that propels social scientists in the developing countries to rise in revolt and raise their voice against academic imperialism.

The universalist assumption of social sciences, as Kothari puts it, is based on "a blind acceptance of the predictive model of physical sciences (which itself is based on an inadequate understanding of the scientific process) which do not admit of normative consideration of the ends of human endeavour and the means to achieve these ends. Social science paradigms essentially means paradigms, the values underlying them essentially means values; what are known as 'models' must of necessity be different for different societies and hence permit human intervention. Yet the methodology is based on absolutist assumption of universalism"[3].

The trend towards "indigenization" or "regionalization" is in a very crucial sense a serious attempt to provide the much needed corrective to the deficiencies in the dominant paradigms of research. We have already referred to the irrelevancy of the attempt to develop a general theory. Even those theories that do not strive to do so suffer from grievous drawbacks. Most of these theories take inspiration from physical sciences and aspire to develop generalizations of universal validity. This aspiration often amounts to "mechanomorphism" since the understanding of the complexities of a social order is based on their reduction to physical and chemical units. Even when an awareness of the complexity of a social order is present, the exploration of this complexity is attempted through the help of multiple variables rather than taking into account the multivariable circumstances of organized complexity.

The movement of "indigenization" and "regionalization" draws attention to these deficiencies of the dominant paradigms and creates environments within which dominant theories and methodologies can be more critically tested, evaluated and improved upon than ever before. It also provides opportunities for genuine international exchange based on a candid confrontation of diverse world views drawn from diverse historical and institutional experiences. Seen in this perspective, such a movement does not pose any threat to universality of knowledge; what it, however, does is to transform the centre-peripheric relationship that exists now into a polycentric world of social sciences. As Alger and Lyons point out:

"The bases - whether they be identified as ideological or simply experiential - on which social scientists make research choices and direct investigations are now complex and diverse. Under the earlier dispensation, the links between social scientists at the centres, however divergent their ideological differences, were cultural, as well as scientific. These links were, however, more tight, the fewer the centres. But as the centres multiply and as those at the former peripheries pursue autonomous routes to theoretical and methodological experiment, the links of a transnational community become more complex and interacting"[4].

The enrichment of social science theories and methodologies through cross-fertilization is dependent also on diffusion of knowledge and co-operation. And this is the third sense in which

(1) See Norman W. Storer, "The Internationality of Science and the Nationality of Scientists" International Social Science Journal, Vol. XXII, No.1 (1970), pp.80-93.
(2) Storer, Ibid., p.82.
(3) Rajni Kothari, op. cit.
(4) Op. cit., p.145.

the term universalism is used. This co-operation has, in view of the evolving pluralism in the transnational system of social sciences, two aspects: co-operation between developing and developed and that between developing and developed countries. Deferring the discussion of co-operation between the developing countries for the next section, two crucial issues seem to be noteworthy in so far as the question of co-operation between developing and developed nations is concerned. In the first place, in spite of the breakdown of dependency relationship between centre and periphery, the asymmetric nature of the transnational system of social sciences still remains a harsh reality.

The greater concentration in the developed nations of resources and infrastructures requisite for a vigorous social science movement is contrasted with the meagre resources allocated to social sciences, the still tradition-bound universities and fewer number of research institutes in the developing countries. This in itself imposes severe constraints on the growth and development of social sciences in the developing world. Any large-scale co-operation in the present stage of the under-developed nature of social sciences in the developing countries is likely to accentuate dependency relations. As Rodolpho A. Bulatao has argued:

"Increasing co-operation under present conditions would only strengthen existing patterns of dependency. It becomes a question of strategy and tempo to move towards greater co-operation only as autonomous centres grow up in developing countries, or through networks of co-operation that help make them autonomous"(1).

In the second place, therefore, there is also the issue of creating and sustaining strong bases for national social sciences to develop and grow. As a matter of fact, the argument can forcefully be made that there cannot be a true international social science community without strong national communities. As Silvert has argued, "Only members of strong national communities have the capacity to participate effectively in international activities"(2). If this is true, and there is no valid ground to believe otherwise, then one of the preconditions of meaningful international co-operation, especially between the developing and the developed nations, is the creation of a critical social science mass in terms of numbers, institutions and standards in the developing countries. Until there is such a critical mass, involvement in transnational activities only maintains dependencies.

But what are the prospects of the creation of such a critical social science mass in the developing countries? If the creation of this critical mass takes long to consummate, what effect will it have on the process of "indigenization" and "regionalization" of social sciences in Asia? And what can be done to speed up the creation of this critical mass? It is to discussing these questions that we now turn.

IV. CONDITIONS AFFECTING INTER-REGIONAL CO-OPERATION IN THE SOCIAL SCIENCES

We talked of turning away from the dominant concepts and theories imported from the West. This has important consequences for development and growth of social sciences in Asian countries. In the first place, it has created a greater awareness of the distinctive rôle that social sciences can play in national development. Inducing social change is not merely a matter of importing technology and plans for speeding up change through the adoption of new techniques. Sole reliance on techniques comes up against obstacles that are irritating precisely because they are not technical. It is for this reason that social scientists are more and more in demand in the developing countries for training administrators and various other categories of personnel and for undertaking research.

In the second place, the enhanced importance of social sciences has, in several Asian countries, led to the establishment of Social Science Research Councils for equivalent bodies in order to formulate social science research policies, co-ordinate and finance research programmes, and build infrastructural facilities for supporting and sustaining research activities. With the setting up of these bodies, determination of priority areas for research has also been undertaken.

And, lastly, the emphasis on the "social usefulness" of social sciences is creating two kinds of pressure. First, this pressure is expressed in the demand of vocational training within higher education. This manifests itself in university social science departments turning more and more to producing social workers, planners and administrators. Second, this pressure is also turning the attention of social scientists to evaluative and diagnostic studies whose primary concerns are to assess the achievement, or lack of it, of particular programmes and find out the reasons for shortfalls. The overall impact of both these pressures is to demonstrate the inadequacy of unidisciplinary perspectives on the phenomenon of social change and the need for integrated social science departments for teaching and transdisciplinary approach to research.

These developments are, no doubt, beneficial. They have created an acute awareness of the deficiencies of the dominant paradigms of social sciences and the traditional structures of higher learning. They have also been instrumental in removing some of the ill-effects of the feeling of inferiority complex of Asian social scientists and fill them with a sense of confidence for recreating social sciences relevant to conditions prevailing in Asian countries.

(1) In Alger and Lyons, op. cit., p. 139.
(2) Ibid., p. 141.

Given these, however, there are certain imbalances that make for uncertainties with respect to "indigenization" and "regionalization" of social sciences in Asia. In the first place, since the "imported" concepts and theories still provide the dominant framework of perception of reality, dependence relations still characterize much of teaching and research in the developing countries. This trend has further been accentuated by the pressures on univeristy departments and research institutes to produce socially useful personnel and research respectively. It is true that the current emphasis on teaching and research on nationally relevant problems does much to reorient social scientists to nationally operative societal processes and promises to yield concepts and theories that are based on national experience. However, this also diverts social science energy away from theoretical and methodological innovations without which truly indigenous social science will not develop. The emphasis on applied social science research tends to maintain the fragmented character of social sciences which, in turn, weakens the advancement of both basic and applied research. Similarly, the necessity to produce trained personnel for handling developmental tasks reduces the autonomy of university departments in a way which undermines their rôle in the important function of innovation in theory and methodology.

In the second place, in addition to a lower resource allocation to social science research, there is also evident in many of the Asian countries a tendency to denigrate the need to produce highly trained professional social scientists or to set up social science research institutes for basic research. This is tantamount to ignoring the creation of the necessary resource base that can support innovative thinking which may really indigenize social sciences in Asia.

What implications does this situation have for co-operation across national boundaries in Asia? It should be clear by now that the existence of strong national social sciences is a precondition for effective and meaningful co-operation in a wider arena. As has been indicated above, the tendency towards "indigenization" reflects an articulation of the need rather than the creation of requisite bases for the fulfilment of that need. As such, the slogan of "indigenization" in many of the developing countries remains an ideological or political posture rather than an academic operational programme. The positive side of the insistence on "indigenization" should not, however, be lost sight of. It has helped in realizing the necessity of articulating national perspectives on social sciences, on the one hand, and emphasized the need to enter into co-operative relationship with other developing countries, on the other.

There exist basically two structures for institutionalized co-operation among the Asian countries. First, there are governmental and non-governmental international agencies that have sponsored and promoted wide varieties of co-operative research programmes. Second, there is institutional co-operation between research institutes and research councils for promoting collaborative cross-national studies and training. Agencies falling under the first category can again be further divided on the basis of their purpose and funding sources. In the first place, there is Unesco itself which is primarily responsible for promoting social science research and teaching. Its main objective is the advancement of social science knowledge, communication and exchange of results of research within the framework of international intellectual co-operation. There is no doubt that Unesco has done quite a lot to promote social sciences in Asia[1]. However, it has to ensure that the programmes adopted reflect the needs of Member States as accurately as possible. Furthermore, its slender resources for the developing countries are barely sufficient to provide for the stimulation and initiation of research at the regional level.

There is a second category of international agencies that have been brought into being by the United Nations or one of its Specialized Agencies or by the United Nations in collaboration with particular government(s). Asian Statistical Institute, Tokyo, United Nations Asian Institute for Economic Development and Planning, Bangkok, United Nations Centre for Regional Development, Nagoya are some of the examples. These agencies are responsible for carrying out research and/or training activities in particular areas of social sciences and have the primary functions of training government officials as well as to render advisory services to the governments in the Asian region.

Apart from these international agencies there have, in the recent years, come up non-governmental organizations, such as, Asian Association of Development Research and Training Institutes and the Association of Asian Social Science Research Councils. However, these organizations are too recent to make any deep impact. Moreover, these organizations have to depend for resources on other funding agencies and/or press their own articulation of priorities on agencies like Unesco for initiation of action.

(1) For an assessment of Unesco's work, see Marie-Anne de Franz, "Implanting the Social Sciences - A Review of Unesco's Endeavours", International Social Science Journal (Paris), Vol. XXI, No. 3, 1969, pp. 406-420. For a discussion of Unesco's programme in Asia, see Unesco, "Priorities for Social Science Research in Developing Countries" (Paris), September 1975, mimeo; for a discussion of Unesco Research Centre on Social and Economic Development in Southern Asia, see Janusz A. Ziolkowski, "Unesco Research Centre on Social and Economic Development in Southern Asia, 1956-1966: A Retrospective View", (n. d.), mimeo.

V. CONCLUDING REMARKS

This discussion highlights some factors that impinge on the development of social sciences in Asian countries and their implications for regional and global co-operation. As was pointed out earlier, the centre-periphery relationship is breaking down and the stress on the necessity to indigenize social sciences has increased. This has also led to a strong perception of regional co-operation matched by some concrete action in this direction. However, two basic constraints affect adversely the prospects of effective and meaningful regional as well as global co-operation in the social sciences. In the first place, if the route to such a co-operation lies through strengthening national social science communities, then certain structural characteristics impede its occurrence. Rigidities of university departments, non-existence of academic centres engaged in the crucial task of theoretical and methodological innovations, paucity of basic resources, such as, trained professional social scientists and funds, etc., are some of the structural characteristics. In the second place, the lack of these basic resources also means that regional organizations may begin with enthusiasm but their enthusiasm wanes when it is realized that funds necessary to implement their programme will not easily be available. ASSRREC is a case in point. The lack of funds also hampers participation of Asian social scientists in transnational social science activities.

All this points to the necessity of ensuring (a) participation of Asian social scientists in transnational social science activities; (b) greater allocation of resources to social science research and development in the Asian countries; (c) availability of academic centres to engage in theoretical and methodological innovations; (d) training of teachers and research scholars capable of undertaking trans-disciplinary teaching and research; and (e) availability of adequate resource base to regional social science organizations.

It is in the context of these needs that international and regional organizations with the responsibility to promote social sciences must gear their activities.

CHAPTER 3

The Latin American Experience and Inter-Regional Co-operation in the Social Sciences

by
Enrique Oteiza

Former Executive Secretary
Latin American Social Science Council

CO-OPERATION AND SOCIAL SCIENCES
DEVELOPMENT IN LATIN AMERICA

1. Introduction

Before entering into a more specific description of
the way co-operation in social science research and
training in Latin America evolved over time, and
into a discussion of its contribution and shortcomings in the process of development of those sciences
in the region, it may be useful to present an overview of what that development has been during the
last decades.

This overview will not explain in detail how
each of the disciplines and problem-oriented interdisciplinary areas of studies developed in organization and content; such a presentation would be beyond
the scope of the present paper. It will rather broadly
illustrate some aspects of the process that give an
indication of how social science activities evolved
in this region.

Since the late forties, when ECLA made its
very significant appearance on the Latin American
scene, the growth of the Latin American social sciences has been rapid. At the end of that decade a
not insignificant group of Latin American social
scientists were, for the first time, studying different
aspects of social processes at national and regional
levels.

From the point of view of research activities,
the growth was fast. The number of research institutes in the social sciences in the region approximately doubled in the fifties and again in the sixties.
By 1975 there were about 80 member research institutes in CLACSO, most of them active and real,
though only a few were large in terms of number
of researchers. This, of course, created a growing demand for social scientists in general, though
economists benefited from it more than other
professions.

With regard to training, there was a rapid development of undergraduate courses in the social
sciences in many Latin American countries, and
some of these programmes were of a fairly good

quality. A minority of those who obtained a first
degree in the social sciences, together with others
coming from the traditional professions, were able
to pursue graduate studies; particularly in universities outside the region, mostly in Europe and the
U. S. A.

It was these social scientists, for the most
part with graduate training outside the region, who
staffed the newly created research institutions and
became professors in Latin American universities.

The demand from academic institutions for
both research and teaching staff grew relatively
fast. By 1970, the community of well-trained social scientists in Latin America had reached a
considerable size. Simultaneously, the demand
from governmental agencies and international organizations in the region also grew, with economists s
again being the preferred profession. Of course,
the situation with regard to research and training
activities in the social sciences differed significantly among the different Latin American countries. Large and medium sized countries in the
region tended to develop bigger structures in the
social sciences than the smaller ones, though
political factors were also important.

In terms of teaching undergraduate programmes
in the different branches of the social sciences
there was, as in the case of research, a significant
expansion during the fifties and sixties. This development took part mostly in the universities of
the region. In many instances it was part of a
wider process of university reform that, among
other changes, involved an increase of scientific
activities - research and training - in both the natural and social sciences.

Since the sixties there has been some expansion
of graduate programmes in the region. New international academic institutions like FLACSO and
CELADE have provided master-level programmes
and have begun to form researchers and university professors in sociology, demography and political science, many of whom went to staff research
institutes and universities throughout Latin America.

National graduate programmes in the social

sciences - in some cases with regional coverage - also emerged during that period at a number of universities and academic institutions in Latin America, such as Escolatina or CIDU in Santiago; CENDES in Venezuela; El Colegio de Mexico and UNAM in Mexico; the Catholic University in Lima; CEUR and Bariloche Foundation in Argentina; Economics at University of Brasilia and Faculty Candido Mendes in Brazil, etc.

The present level of activity in the social sciences is much higher than in 1950, in spite of the very important setbacks. There is a significant amount of research work going on and the effort to replace the training of graduate Latin American students outside the region by relevant and good quality training inside the area continues. CLACSO's Latin American Graduate Training Programme in the Social Sciences has, in the last couple of years, brought together the institutes or centres of the region which have good quality programmes at graduate level, and where research and training are well integrated.

Reference has been made here to academic institutions, social scientists, and research and teaching programmes. These have been mentioned as a way of illustrating a process of growth and decline, and the existence of some difficulties, as a background for what will be presented in the coming sections about collaboration. It should be added that parallel to this process, and as a result of it, the social sciences in Latin America have shown a very noticeable substantive development. The quantity and quality of work and its relevance have contributed significantly towards a better understanding of Latin American history and the nature of the processes that explain its underdevelopment. While making this contribution, Latin American social sciences have produced important notions and perspectives with regard to development problems in general.

To put this brief general presentation into a proper perspective some weaknesses in the way the Latin American social sciences have developed during the last three decades should also be pointed out. These are mainly a sort of sub-aspect of the more general dependency type of situation that exists in the region.

First of all there is a lack of adequate local support to sustain the degree and type of research and teaching structure needed in view of the longer term genuine development of Latin American societies. The counterpart to this is an excessive dependency on foreign financial sources, which tends to distort priorities and impose perspectives which are not always relevant locally.

Secondly, there is still an insufficient development of high quality, relevant graduate training programmes in the social sciences, thus making the reproduction and expansion of the present stock of Latin American social scientists excessively dependent on advance training outside the area. The effect of this type of training in terms of alienation,

stimulus to the brain drain and irrelevance is well experienced and known in the region. This weakness is in part due to the crisis of the Latin American university, which in turn is a result of a much broader socio-political crisis.

Finally, there is an inadequate academic infrastructure in terms of libraries, documentation, information systems, archives and data banks. Even at the relatively simple and more traditional level of libraries, the most important Latin American collections are outside the region.

2. Intra-regional Latin American collaboration in the social sciences

In spite of the fact that progress in the social sciences was already considerable, by 1960 it began to be perceived clearly that more formal and permanent mechanisms of collaboration at a regional level were needed. The number of regional, and particularly national, research and training institutions was multiplying fast, but there was little systematic contact and discussion among researchers working on similar topics; lack of information about ongoing research in the area; poor circulation of works produced by the different institutes; and almost a complete absence of collaborative research projects. Collaboration was also non-existent with regard to training programmes in the social sciences.

On the other hand very strong institutional links between Latin American research institutions and parent academic institutions in the U.S.A. and Western Europe persisted, while the "alma mater" connexions between Latin American social scientists and universities outside the region were too strong.

It is possible to say that there was too much of a centrifugal type of connexion with academic institutions in the U.S.A. and Western Europe, and simultaneously almost a complete lack of adequate mechanisms for intra-regional co-operation.

For about five years - from 1960 to 1965 - there was discussion first and preparatory work later in order to establish some type of institution that could organize a permanent collaborative network in Latin America, bringing together institutions and persons working in the social sciences. Different opinions were analysed, such as basing the institution to be created on a federation of the national professional disciplinary associations in existence in some of the countries; or on an association of university research and teaching units in the social sciences (schools, departments, faculties, institutes); or bringing together the research units, independently of their institutional affiliation (whether they are located in universities or not, etc.).

A final decision was made in the course of the preliminary consultation and organizational process in favour of associating Latin American research institutions. In this way it was possible to find a fairly wide base both in terms of disciplinary and geographical coverage. The research units option permitted the exclusion of traditional groups that existed in Latin America and were not research oriented (purely teaching ones or the more juridical or philosophically oriented in the old-fashioned tradition that existed in the area).

The creation of the Latin American Social Science Council (CLACSO) was the result of the above-mentioned process. It was formally established by decision of the representatives of 32 research institutions from the area, which in turn became the first member centres of the Council. Its main purpose is to contribute to the development of the social sciences in Latin America and to the strengthening of the institutions dedicated to research and training in those sciences.

In terms of organization, CLACSO is governed by a General Assembly made up of representatives of the Member Centres (presently 80). The General Assembly is required to meet at least every two years and apart from discussing and approving the programme and budget of the Council, elects an Executive Committee of 18 members for a period of four years, in which a balance between the countries of the region and the disciplines of the social sciences is aimed at. An Executive Secretary is also appointed by the General Assembly for a period of four years in order to implement the decisions made by the Assembly and the Executive Committee and take care of permanent activities.

A more detailed list of CLACSO's objectives includes the following main items:

- improve and stimulate scientific communication within the region and co-operation among the Council's member centres;
- promote basic and applied research in the different fields of the social sciences, and research and training projects of particular importance to Latin America;
- stimulate the continuous improvement of teaching and training in the social sciences in Latin America;
- assist in the mobility of social scientists within the region, and contribute to a better use of the human academic resources available in Latin America;
- promote the study of Latin American integration;
- develop academic co-operation with other areas of the world, particularly Asia and Africa.

The Council's key instruments for developing collaboration in research on a regional basis are its working commissions. These are decentralized collaborative research efforts bringing together active researchers in the fields of knowledge on which the commissions are focused. Each commission has a co-ordinator or group leader, who must be a well-established scientist in the corresponding field of study, and who must devote a substantial amount of time to that activity. At present, the following working commissions are in existence:

- Economic History
- Urban and Regional Development
- Studies on Dependency
- Rural Studies
- Science, Technology and Development
- Population and Development
- Studies on the State
- Education and Development
- Labour Movements.

Besides these working commissions, there are working groups established to tackle problems which appear to be important but are just beginning to be considered under a collaborative approach by Latin American social scientists and centres related to CLACSO. A Working Group on Income Distribution (which may later develop into commission) is functioning, while more preliminary work is being done in connexion with the creation of other ones.

In addition to the collaborative research effort, CLACSO has developed a Latin American Graduate Training Programme in the Social Sciences in order to tackle the urgent need to raise the standards of graduate training in the social sciences in the region. The approach has consisted of establishing a regional system of advanced studies in those sciences by improving and regionalizing existing national programmes, making better use of the few existing regional ones and developing others in field or sub-regions which are not properly covered. This Latin American Graduate Training Programme is presently receiving support from Unesco, UNDP and other agencies, particularly with regard to the development of a pool of scholarships in order to select and assign properly good Latin American students to the best places in the region. Also the existing support permits the mobilization of teaching staff in the area through visiting professorship schemes as well as the promotion of permanent exchanges and discussion about content, orientation and organization of the training programmes incorporated into the system. In advance training it can also be said, as in the case of research, that CLACSO's Latin American intra-regional collaborative experience in the social sciences has proved to be valuable.

The organization of the Council as a Latin American academic institution has permitted the member centres, collectively, to have a voice and define science policy at a regional Latin American level. Before, the supra-national regional dimension in organizing social science activities was the privilege of institutions and governments located outside Latin America. CLACSO's working commissions and groups can now define research priorities from within Latin America, and decide how to fund the projects or negotiate funds. Something similar has occurred in graduate training.

The consequence, therefore, of organization at the intra-regional level has been a redefinition of inter-regional patterns of co-operation[1]. In this respect the Latin American social sciences are far from having eliminated the unbalanced situation in their academic relations with the U.S.A. and Western Europe, but the conditions have improved, allowing a relatively more symmetric collaboration. Exchanges and collaboration with Asia and Africa are still very weak, though there has been some progress thanks to the effort made by the respective regional associations and the support of some agencies (Unesco, OECD Development Centre and IDRC).

Though CLACSO has been the collaborative Latin American institution par excellence be cause of its objectives and structure, many other national and regional institutions have played a not insignificant rôle in this collective Latin American effort. Among the regional United Nations agencies, ECLA and CELADE have played an important rôle. FLACSO, a purely Latin American intergovernmental academic institution, has contributed a lot to the development of the social sciences in the region, mostly through its regional graduate training programmes. In the past these were devoted to sociology and political sciences, but they are now being expanded both disciplinarily and regionally.

3. Some specific characteristics of social science research in Latin America

The emergence of the Latin American social sciences on the international intellectual scene is marked by a number of distinct characteristics, some of which have relatively deep historical roots. Among them, several deserve mention.

As a society, and as a culture, Latin America is marked by the superimposition during a very long period of European colonial domination from Spain and Portugal over pre-Colombian societies and civilizations. There was abundant immigration from Europe, which provided the population for the dominant upper classes, and from Africa, that through the institution of slavery supplied a population to be exploited in addition to the preexisting, so-called "Indians". A mark was left culturally from this combination of populations of very different origins during several centuries of colonial rule. This historical process, resulted in a peculiar type of socio-economic formation with a powerful land-owning class and enclaves of a plantation and mineral exploitation type linked with markets abroad, which have contributed to the formation of some persistent characteristics of Latin American societies; it is what has been called the "colonial heritage" of the region.

During the long colonial period and after "independence" (last century) until now, the continent has been gradually and increasingly incorporated in a subordinate rôle into the process of expansion and evolution of the capitalistic system.

The nature of Latin American social sciences can be better understood if this background, which was referred to briefly only to provide some perspective, is kept in mind. It is the structural characteristics of Latin American societies that have been shaped in a specific way over the past centuries - its present "dependent" nature - that permit some insights with regard to the constraints and possibilities of the Latin American social sciences.

The evolution of social sciences in the region is conditioned to some extent by socio-economic structures that perpetuate power in the hands of social groups that need very little in terms of local scientific creativity in order to maintain or enlarge their interests. Their insertion in a broader transnational system makes them dependent on foreign, not domestic, knowledge. This explains the very low level of material support provided for scientific activities in general, which is reflected in weak structures of research.

There is nevertheless a difference between the more industrialized countries in Latin America and the rest. The former, even if also economically dependent, require more in terms of local social science than the latter. It is the special nature of the knowledge required in the case of the more industrialized countries of the region that has produced a demand for the more "technocratic" type of social scientist, mostly economists of neoclassical orientation, though there is also some room for acritical sociologists. This category of social scientists is known in some Latin American countries as technobureaucrats, and is supposedly "apolitical".

The very weak situation in terms of scientific institutions and socio-economic conditioning has been aggravated in the last ten years by an almost chronic crisis of the universities in a number of countries in the region, as a result of conflicts which are a part of a much broader socio-political crisis.

In spite of these unfavourable conditions, there has been a very significant development of the social sciences in the region in the last three decades, as has been seen before, with not only growth in the magnitude of research and training activities, but, furthermore, progress in terms of relevance, creativity and quality.

Here is where the Latin American experience seems to be particularly relevant with regard to regional collaboration. It has been the relatively high level of collaboration by comparison with other regions that has permitted Latin American social scientists and institutions to overcome partially the limitations stemming from the structure

(1) On this matter see "New Forms of Collaboration in Development Research and Training"; by Samir Amin, Giulio Fossi, Richard Jolly, Enrique Oteiza, Poona Wignaraja; International Social Science Journal, Unesco, Paris, June 1975.

of local societies and their subordinate nature in terms of foreign dependency.

Active intra-regional collaboration facilitated communication among social scientists, ideas circulated fast, information flew and discussion took place. Publication and distribution schemes contributed positively to this process, facilitated by a linguistic situation where only two similar languages are the predominant vehicles for internal social science production. Collaborative programmes contributed to the advancement of research and accumulation of knowledge in the region, and they were also important for the improvement of graduate training. Existing resources were optimized partly because of collaboration, and this allowed severe limitations to be overcome.

The tension between indigenization of Latin American social sciences and the heavy weight of the structures of dependency is high. Excessive need of foreign financial support, because of an extreme lack of Latin American finance, and for foreign training tend to perpetuate the distortion and consequently create tension, once Latin American social scientists have acquired consciousness with regard to this problem.

Much can be obtained in the future from collaboration in augmenting the relevance of scientific work. Working commissions can increase their influence in the processes that lead to the setting of research priorities and the development of adequate perspectives for the creation of new knowledge. Collaboration in training can also contribute to relevance by facilitating organization of academic resources and improving the content, orientation and quality of training programmes.

4.   Possibilities and constraints for future
      international collaboration in the
      social sciences

The experience of intra-regional collaboration in the social sciences, in the last decades, proves that very significant academic work can be carried on as a result of it. Thus collaboration in this field is feasible. What really makes the feasibility of collaboration in social sciences important is that research, communication, teaching and science policy activities conducted in this way have proved to be of great benefit, at least in the case of Latin America.

There are now regional institutions especially devoted to intra-regional collaboration (CLACSO, CODESRIA, EADI, and ADIPA) in Africa, Asia, Europe and Latin America. Their success should reflect also in a redefinition of inter-regional academic exchanges and collaboration, particularly by transforming the present unbalanced, patterns into better-balanced ones.

The constraints which limit intra-regional collaboration in the social sciences, in the Third World regions, have already been mentioned. Firstly, there are socio-economic conditioning factors that result in a lack of an adequate scientific research and educational structure (lack of support and resources, inadequate institutional set-up, lack of continuity, lack of information, etc.). Secondly, repressive pro-status quo governments in many Third World countries tend to perceive social science as a danger inasmuch as in its more critical and socially committed version it reveals the mechanisms of domination and exploitation and the forms of insertion in the international system that are the very root of poverty and underdevelopment. By sad experience it is well known how this form of repression affects the work of social scientists and decreases the possibilities of collaboration. Thirdly, lack of local funds and the corresponding excessive dependence on extra-regional funds, plus too much advanced training in Europe and the U.S.A. and not enough available within the Third World regions, contribute to perpetuate unbalanced academic relations as well as to stimulate a significant proportion of irrelevant academic work. Fourthly, obstacles to freedom of circulation of persons, as well as of published materials, are increasing in some of the Third World areas. Certainly these obstacles in circulation create a structural barrier to communication, which works in itself against the possibilities of collaboration.

When it comes to inter-regional collaboration in the social sciences, the difficulties become much greater. "Collaboration" between underdeveloped and developed regions is substantial, but it is of the wrong sort. A lot has been said and written about the problems of academic imperialism, lack of symmetry or unbalanced flows of exchange, scientific dependence and one-way transfers of knowledge, wrong procedures for the definition of research priorities and the irrelevance and inadequacy of training outside the regions. It is not necessary to develop this question here as it is well treated in the previously-mentioned paper on "New Forms of Collaboration"(1).

On the other hand, academic collaboration between Asia, Africa and Latin America has been traditionally non-existent. The colonial linkages and contemporary forms of insertion of the countries of these regions in the world economic, political and cultural system has shaped solid centre-periphery type networks and not connected the regions in the periphery to each other.

There are, thus, hard obstacles to be overcome in order to establish adequate academic exchanges and co-operation between the Third World Regions. The most notorious are the following. Lack of social scientists in Africa, Asia

(1) On this matter see "New Forms of Collaboration in Development Research and Training"; by Samir Amin, Giulio Fossi, Richard Jolly, Enrique Oteiza, Poona Wignaraja; International Social Science Journal, Unesco, Paris, June 1975.

and Latin America with sufficient knowledge about the history and problems of development of other regions of the Third World outside their own. This is the result of the lack of specialized programmes for this purpose in those regions, including the lack of scholarships and other means adequate for this type of exchange and training. Also there is a lack of an adequate system for the permanent diffusion and circulation of books, journals and the products of academic work between regions; this is aggravated by the insufficient proportions of research production in social sciences in the Third World which is translated and published so that it can be of use in other regions. In a more general level it is amazing the lack of resources that international organizations and governments channel into programmes of exchange and collaboration between Third World regions.

As in the case of the already successful examples of intra-regional collaboration in the social sciences (i.e. some of the Regional Associations), much can be expected from an effort to establish stable forms of collaboration between research and training institutes of the different Third World regions, in the social sciences and among social scientists working on similar topics. The understanding of problems of underdevelopment and how to overcome them can be broadened and improved by these exchanges, and collaboration in academic activities should stimulate a mutual learning process. There are obvious advantages with regard to improving the knowledge about the processes going on in the central capitalistic countries, the industrialized socialist countries, and in general the international system (economic, political and otherwise).

Another special aspect of inter-regional collaboration in the social sciences is the relatively weak nature of the exchanges between most Third World countries and European Socialist countries. Again a number of barriers are imposed in many cases to institutions or scientists wanting to engage in some sort of collaboration at this level. There is thus ample room and need to eliminate barriers in the Third World countries and elsewhere and establish adequate mechanisms of balanced academic exchange and collaboration.

5. Recommendations

From what has been said in previous sections of this paper, several recommendations emerged as important. These concern mostly international and regional organizations which are already involved in programmes of exchanges and collaboration in the social sciences at intra- and inter-regional levels, such as Unesco and the other United Nations agencies, the International Social Science Council and the international disciplinary associations in the social sciences, the regional associations (CLACSO, CODESRIA, EADI and ADIPA), the OECD Development Centre, etc. Some national institutions who play an international academic rôle (such as IDRC of Canada and National Social Science Councils in a number of countries) should, in principle, be also concerned with the improvement and better balancing of the intra- and inter-regional co-operative effort. The following will be mentioned.

(a) Assign resources in order to reinforce inter-regional collaboration in research between Third World regions.

(b) Establish scholarships programmes in order to train some Third World social science graduate students in underdeveloped regions outside their own (i.e. African students in Asia and Latin America, and so on).

(c) Reassign resources so as to allow the exchange of visiting professors and researchers within the Third World regions.

(d) Establish translations and publications programmes in order to ensure that research done in one Third World region is available in the language of other underdeveloped regions (this involves mostly translation from Spanish and Portuguese into English and French, as social scientists in Latin America are in less need because in most cases they can read the four languages).

(e) Distribute regularly relevant publications that come out in one region to the libraries of the main academic institutions of the other regions.

(f) Support good Third World journals.

(g) Support the information services on research and training institutions and ongoing research of the type that has been done by the OECD Development Centre.

(h) Support inter-regional seminars like the Afro-Latin American one that took place at IDEP (Dakar) a few years ago with Unesco's backing.

(i) Support inter-regional meetings organized as much as possible by, or jointly with, the respective regional associations.

(j) Revise the mechanism for defining research priorities so that relevant regional and local academic institutions participate effectively.

(k) Reinforce, in general, programmes for graduate training in the social sciences inside the Third World regions.

(l) Defend the rights of social scientists to carry on with their work and defend human rights and dignity, and social justice in general.

(m) Promote free circulation of social scientists, which is indispensable for academic work.

(n) Establish inter-regional co-operation in a balanced and symmetrical form (avoid academic imperialism in its different forms).

(o) Verify that each collaborative project contributes towards the reinforcement of local institutions in the Third World, so that dependency is less at the end of the project or programme than at the beginning.

SHORT BIBLIOGRAPHY ON LATIN AMERICAN SOCIAL SCIENCES AND COLLABORATION

Samir Amin, Giulio Fossi, Richard Jolly, Enrique Oteiza, Poona Wignaraja; New Forms of Collaboration in Development Research and Training; International Social Science Journal, No. 4 1975, pp. 710-795, Paris.

Ivan Francisco Marsal; La Investigación Sociológica en América Latina; Papers, Volumen I; Universidad Autónoma de Barcelona, 1973.

Octavio Ianni; Sociologia de Sociologia Latino-Americana; Civilização Brasileira, 2e Ediçao, Río de Janeiro 1976.

I. L. Horowitz; The Rise and Fall of Project Camelot; The M. I. T. Press, Cambridge, Mass. 1967.

Gino Germani; La Sociología en América Latina, EUDEBA, Buenos Aires, 1964.

Florestán Fernández; O padrao de trabalho Científico dos Sociologos Brasileiros; Revista Brasileira de Estudos Politicos, Minas Gerais, 1958.

Orlando Fals Borda; Ciencia Propia y Colonialismo Intelectual; Editorial Nuestro Tiempo, México, 1970.

Pablo González Casanova y Guillermo Bonfil; Las Ciencias Sociales y la Antropología; en Ediciones Productividad, México, 1968.

FLACSO, El Papel de la FLACSO en los Estudios sobre el Desarrollo Económico; documento de trabajo presentado al Seminario sobre "Resistencia al Cambio", Río de Janeiro, Octubre 1959.

CLACSO, Memorias Anuales y Boletines, 1968 a 1976.

Jorge Graciarena, La Enseñanza de las Ciencias Sociales en América Latina, Editorial Paidós, Buenos Aires, 1974.

CHAPTER 4

Social Science Co-operation in Africa

by

Mpekesa Bongoy

Centre for Co-ordination of Social Science Research and
Documentation in Africa South of the Sahara, Kinshasa

INTRODUCTION

The area south of the Sahara comprises more than
40 countries, most of them independent and members of Unesco. Each of them generally posseses
at least one university and two social science research institutes. The area is now estimated to
have a total population of over 200 million of which
more than 90% are Africans.

This report covers the following 4 items: a
brief survey of inter-regional co-operation in the
social sciences in Africa south of the Sahara, some
outstanding features of social science research in
the region, possibilities and difficulties in the field
of co-operation and, finally, a few suggestions and
recommendations of a general nature.

SECTION 1 - A BRIEF SURVEY

1. Most of the independent African countries
south of the Sahara have been sovereign States for
only 15 years at the most (as a result of the surge
towards independence in the 1960's). Generally
speaking, the infrastructure set up by the colonial
authorities was oriented towards and integrated
with the infrastructure of the colonizing country in
various fields including economic, technical and
academic organization. This meant that, as a rule,
social science research institutes and organizations
established in Africa were integrated with those in
the colonizing countries and were used either as
sources of basic data for processing in the mother
country or as training grounds for young foreign research workers. The activities of these research
institutions and organizations were not primarily
aimed at seeking ways and means of improving the
social condition of the inhabitants of the colonized
countries. In fact the contrary was often the case
and some of the social research carried out was
designed to obtain better knowledge of the psychological, temperamental, economic and other weaknesses of the inhabitants in order to accentuate these
weaknesses and so perpetuate the stranglehold and

domination of the colonial power. There are countless examples of this type of study and one is consequently obliged to admit their existence as a
historical fact.

As research institutes and organizations in
any colony were offshoots of those in the mother
country, co-operation was obviously vertical between the colony and the colonizing country and
back to the colony, and not horizontal, as between
a French colony and a British or Belgian one.

2. African countries south of the Sahara have
only been independent for a relatively short period
during which they have often been a prey to all sorts
of upheavals such as military coups d'état, seces-
sions, revolts and political troubles ending in
bloodshed. This means that they have not all had
time to amend all the basic structures of their
economic, technical, scientific and academic systems. Worse, neo-colonialist forces have often
encouraged and taken advantage of troubled situations in order to infiltrate into Africa and consolidate certain colonial structures with interests outside the continent. This has been very obvious in
the field of social science research and co-operation
concerning which some African countries have been
induced to sign bilateral co-operation and technical
assistance agreements with ex-colonial powers,
guaranteeing and perpetuating the existing bonds
between the centre and the periphery.

Such agreements have often been followed by
the dispatch to Africa of large numbers of foreign
research workers, and the subjects chosen for research have not always coincided with the fundamental preoccupations of the African governments concerned. Furthermore, foreign research workers
have been entirely or chiefly responsible for much
of the research work done, to the detriment of
African researchers, and this is still the case.

Quite clearly, the perpetuation of preferential
ties of this kind and the fact that national research
workers are inadequately associated with research
activities in their own countries are not factors
conducive to co-operation between research institutes and organizations situated in the area under
study.

3. Various attempts have been made quite recently to establish co-operation between African social science research institutes. Some of the ties existing between research institutes in the East African community consisting of Kenya, Tanzania and Uganda, go back to well before the days of independence. In addition, however, it is worth mentioning the efforts made by CODESRIA, OAU and CERDAS to promote contact between African research workers so that they can decide, jointly and on their own initiative, the topics for multi- and interdisciplinary research.

These three organizations are working to encourage and co-ordinate research and training activities, particularly in the social field, through the medium of the relevant African professional bodies and institutions.

Co-operation between these associations and bodies should find practical expression in:

(1) the exchange and dissemination of information on research and training, including information on personnel, research being planned or in progress, training and refresher course programmes, etc. ;
(2) the translation of important foreign-language texts into African languages such as Swahili, etc. ;
(3) the execution of research projects by several Africans working together in integrated groups of researchers;
(4) the organization of conferences and workshops on subjects of common interest; and
(5) the publication of documents reporting on the work of these integrated research groups.

An association was recently set up to consolidate co-operation among certain African research workers. It is called the Association africaine de sciences politiques (A. A. S. P.) and was founded at Dar es Salaam in December 1973 by 32 African political science experts representing different types of institution (universities, public administration institutes, etc.) in the five main regions of Africa. Although many national political science organizations, e. g. the Nigerian Political Science Association were in existence before A. A. S. P. , the new association fills an awkward gap. Among its objectives are the maintenance of a high standard of research and education, the encouragement of co-operation between research workers and scientists in Africa, the dissemination of the findings of research into problems of crucial interest for Africa, the promotion of co-operation and collaboration with national leaders and those responsible for implementing the various political decisions of African governments, etc.

To sum up, co-operation and collaboration in the social sciences over a territory as vast as Africa south of the Sahara is a fairly new and unfamiliar phenomenon, but the growing realization by African research workers and especially African leaders of the positive part that the social sciences

can and should play in development planning means that prospects for the future are quite bright. At the same time, however, various restrictive factors must necessarily moderate this optimism, as will be seen further on.

SECTION 2 - SOME OUTSTANDING FEATURES OF SOCIAL SCIENCE RESEARCH IN AFRICA SOUTH OF THE SAHARA

In the recent, colonial past, the social sciences in African countries belonging to CERDAS were completely dominated by social science imported from the West, especially from France, England, Germany and Belgium. This applied equally to research and other activities in this field. This is why the favourite subjects of research were cultural anthropology, musicology, traditional ways of life, etc., and research workers mostly seemed to take malicious pleasure in studying and writing about certain aspects of the so-called rough, barbarbarous life of the natives. Most of this research tended to do no more than describe a situation, and was therefore not directed to solving the problems of the people who had been the subject of the investigations.

Moreover, as we have already pointed out, the people in charge of this research were foreigners, living in Africa for a fixed period and having secure positions and salaries in their country of origin.

At present, although Western-oriented research is still being carried out in Africa, there is an increasing tendency towards:

(a) Africanization of research; and
(b) a choice of subjects of research connected with the solution of practical problems.

AFRICANIZATION

The trend towards Africanization may be observed in two spheres: first as regards the problems to be dealt with, which concern local populations and more especially the rural environments in which over 70% of the population still live, and secondly, with respect to African research workers.

One finds that African social science research institutes and organizations are endeavouring to give priority to subjects which are relevant to rural living and which should lead to the solution of certain real and specific problems. This can be seen just by reading the list of priority research projects selected by IRES, NISER, ISSER, IPD, CODESRIA, CERDAS and others.

Many of these projects were either suggested by governments or were based on current governmental preoccupations.

As regards the integration of "indigenous" research workers into social science research activities in Africa, CERDAS, CODESRIA, NISER and many other organizations are anxious to see Africans, alone or in partnership with certain non-Africans, carry out research on Africa. At the conference recently organized in Alexandria by Unesco and WHO and attended by many research workers from Africa south of the Sahara, one important resolution dealt with the indigenization of research and the rôle of local scientists in research activities. It was clearly stated that no research could be carried out in Africa without the participation of a certain proportion of African research workers.

Many African countries have a central research organization grouping various national research workers and co-ordinating their activities. Normally, these organizations give their nationals priority in carrying out research work and insist that the data obtained be treated on the spot and kept in the country. The Institut de recherches scientifiques (I. R. S.) in Zaire is headed by a senior civil servant, or high commissioner, appointed by the President of the Republic. One of the aims of I. R. S. is the Africanization of research both as regards its methods and topics and as regards those responsible for carrying it out. The Institut is also responsible for seeing that the most effective use is made of the results of research done by national research workers. In Cameroon, the Office national de la recherche scientifique et technique (ONAREST) performs the same functions as I. R. S. in Zaire.

SECTION 3 - THE POSSIBILITIES FOR CO-OPERATION AND DIFFICULTIES ENCOUNTERED

Section 3.1. As emphasized above, co-operation is possible between the various African social science research institutes firstly because many African research workers and governments wish and even ask for it and secondly because such co-operation is highly feasible from the technical point of view and from that of infrastructure.

However, various difficulties and restrictions should be mentioned such as difficulties of language and communication, differing scientific backgrounds, the negative attitude sometimes displayed by national authorities towards social science and its part in planning African development, the inadequacy or lack of suitable financial and technical resources, inherited from the colonial and neo-colonial relationship between "peripheral" Africa and the "central" former mother countries, difficulties arising from poor communications between the various African research centres, etc.

All these difficulties and restrictions exist but they can be minimized on the medium term and certainly in the long term. In any case they cannot discourage efforts to hasten co-operation between social scientists and/or social science research organizations in the region south of the Sahara.

Co-operation between the various research institutes and social science research workers in this area may be greatly facilitated by two pan-African organizations: CODESRIA and CERDAS.

CODESRIA

The Conseil pour le développement de la recherche économique et sociale en afrique (CODERESA in French and CODESRIA in English - Council for the Development of Economic and Social Research in Africa) was set up in Dakar in January 1973. CODESRIA's main objective is "to promote research and training activities in the fields of economic and social development in Africa through close co-operation and collaboration among African institutions and professional associations".

CODESRIA aims to reach this praiseworthy overall goal by the following means:

(a) exchange and dissemination of information relating to research and training activities, especially information on staff, research projects on hand or under consideration, and training programmes;

(b) promoting translation into African or other languages as the case may be, of important publications and documents available only in foreign languages;

(c) promoting collaboration in research and training activities, both among institutions in the African region, and between these institutions and similar institutions in other developing and developed areas;

(d) assisting in the development of particular research and training programmes in institutions of the region and helping to secure the necessary assistance from within and outside the region;

(e) organizing working groups, seminars and conferences on subjects of mutual interest; and, finally,

(f) issuing publications relevant to the activities of the Council.

CODESRIA has two categories of members, full and associate.

Full members are national, sub-regional and regional institutions engaged on research related to economic and social development (an essential requirement) and training activities (not imperative). The following are some examples:

the Institut de recherches économiques et sociales (I. R. E. S.) in Zaire, a national research organization attached to the Faculté des sciences économiques of Zaire National University, Kinshasa Campus;

the East Africa Academy of Science, a sub-regional organization;

the Institut panafricain de développement (I.P.D.), a regional organization.

Only full members have the right to vote at CODESRIA meetings.

Other African and foreign research and training

institutions may become associate members. In African countries where such institutions do not yet exist, the Executive Committee of CODESRIA may invite any other organizations willing to undertake research and/or training work to join CODESRIA as associate members.

CODESRIA obtains, or should obtain, its resources in the following way:

annual membership fees;
contributions from African and non-African
  governments;
grants from various international foundations and
  private organizations;
donations from individuals or institutions; and
revenue from the publication of research and from
  other services rendered by CODESRIA. The organization emphasizes, however, that "in all cases, contributions, donations and grants shall be accepted by the Executive Committee provided the conditions are consistent with the maintenance of the integrity and independence of the Council".

CODESRIA's field of action extends over the entire African continent. It is not an intergovernmental organization and may be compared with those independent organizations in Asia and Latin America which work to strengthen scientific co-operation between various research bodies and research workers in those continents.

Since its foundation, CODESRIA has had its headquarters with IDEP in Dakar and has been financed by CRDI, a Canadian organization, but it is now trying to establish its headquarters elsewhere. In December 1975 the Executive Committee decided that CODESRIA should sever its physical and economic ties with IDEP. Among African capitals, Addis Ababa, Yaoundé and Lomé have been mentioned as possible sites for the administrative services of CODESRIA.

Under the vigorous leadership of its First Executive Secretary, Dr. Abdalla S. Bujra, CODESRIA has already organized several working groups in various parts of Africa and is now publishing brief reports summarizing the work of these meetings. CODESRIA will soon start a Newsletter to form a link between research workers and institutes throughout the continent.

CODESRIA's activities are complementary to those of CERDAS. Before considering the relations between these two important organizations whose efforts to encourage social science in Africa seem of prime importance, we shall say something about CERDAS.

CERDAS

CERDAS was founded on 23 September 1974, being set up with Unesco's assistance at the express request of the African Member States of the Organization.

The principal objective of CERDAS is "to promote regional co-operation between institutions of social science research and documentation in Africa south of the Sahara, and to contribute to the development of the social sciences. The centre will devote itself to improving the contribution of the social sciences to the development efforts being carried out in the region, employing all those forms of fundamental and applied research which aim to acquire knowledge of social realities and to develop interdisciplinary, action-oriented methodologies, and carrying out research and documentation co-ordination activities at regional level".

The Acting Director was appointed in 1974 and has his office at CERDAS headquarters in Kinshasa. During the organization's 17 months of existence special efforts have been made to set up a suitable documentation department and an efficient administrative infrastructure, to continue to give encouragement to research workers and to the research previously started under the direct aegis of Unesco and, finally, to inform various States, universities and research institutes in Africa south of the Sahara of the existence of CERDAS and its objectives, and ask them for effective and practical collaboration.

In August 1975 CERDAS convened a meeting in Kinshasa of the directors of research groups in African rural and urban areas. This research is being carried out by Africans of different nationalities in the following countries: Kenya, Tanzania, Ethiopia, Ivory Coast, Cameroon and Zaire (research workers in Ghana and Togo had to abandon their research before it was finished for reasons beyond their control). The bonds forged during this meeting in Kinshasa last August will speed up and strengthen co-operation between the researchers who attended, and various evidence exists to confirm this claim.

The Acting Director of CERDAS and the Executive Secretary of CODESRIA have twice visited several African countries in order to:

make CERDAS more widely known;
ask for moral, material and financial support;
  and
establish a clear distinction between CERDAS and
  CODESRIA on the one hand and CERDAS and
  other African research organizations on the other.
  This last point was particularly pertinent as
  many possibilities of confusion were thus avoided.

The first CERDAS mission (6 September - 4 October 1975) took the two consultants to the following countries: Ethiopia, Kenya, Tanzania, Nigeria, Ghana, Togo, Benin, Ivory Coast and Senegal. The second mission (11 February - 7 March 1976) took them to Uganda, Kenya, Zambia, Tanzania, Ethiopia, Cameroon and Gabon. The CERDAS programme for 1977-1980 provides for similar missions to African countries south of the Sahara which have not yet been visited.

Both these missions enabled CERDAS to make direct contact with ministries of education, vice-chancellors of universities, directors of research institutes, deans, professors, research workers, librarians, and so on. They also enabled the documentation department of CERDAS to be rapidly supplied with documents and publications produced in Africa by African organizations. The CERDAS documentation centre collects documents in English and French. It thus hopes to be of use to English-and French-speaking researchers who wish to come to Kinshasa to spend some time at CERDAS. Breaking down the language barrier can only increase and enrich collaboration and co-operation between African research workers.

CERDAS' long-term programme will shortly be submitted to the CERDAS Governing Board (10-14 May 1976) for examination, as will the budget, so it does not seem very appropriate to "put the cart before the horse". Suffice it to say that Unesco has so far made $60,000 + 80,500 = $140,500 available to CERDAS. Zaire has undertaken to pay 50% of the CERDAS budget and has already contributed $60,000 to the organization. Togo has given 500,000 CFA and Senegal 400,000 CFA. These two countries, with Zaire and Unesco, form the Governing Board of CERDAS. Some of the countries visited by the two CERDAS missions are expected to provide the organization with funds by May 1976 and will thus take part in the centre's forthcoming Administrative Board meeting.

CERDAS-CODESRIA relations

CERDAS is an intergovernmental organization whereas CODESRIA is not.

CODESRIA covers the whole of Africa whereas CERDAS is only concerned with Africa south of the Sahara, although this region has a larger area and population than the part of the continent north of the Sahara. It may be mentioned that the latter region is served by a centre resembling CERDAS, the Arab Centre, which also includes non-African Arab countries.

The two main aspects of CERDAS' activities consist of documentation and co-ordination of research. CODESRIA does not appear to lay stress on documentation. In fact, the Executive Committee decided in December 1974 to ask its Executive Secretary to hand over the CODESRIA data bank to CERDAS and to leave in the hands of CERDAS the principal social science documentation activities. This decision, taken as part of measures to establish co-operation with CERDAS, aimed to avoid costly and inefficient duplication.

As for research, neither CERDAS nor CODESRIA can exhaust individually all the important research topics of interest to African governments and institutions because personnel and financial restrictions make this impossible. It has been suggested that research groups might be led, co-ordinated and financed by CERDAS and CODESRIA as joint ventures in order to strengthen collaboration between these two pan-African organizations. Finally, the suggestion has been made that CODESRIA

should take over international fund-raising while CERDAS would appeal to African governments asking them above all to contribute substantial financial support.

After the first CERDAS mission (August-September 1975), a report was drawn up by Professor M. Bongoy, Acting Director of CERDAS, and Dr. A. S. Bujra, Executive Secretary of CODESRIA, proposing guidelines for co-operation between CERDAS and CODESRIA. Among other things the report states that:

"The two regional organizations are complementary and should consequently collaborate very closely. We suggest the following fields of co-operation:

1. CERDAS and CODESRIA should avoid duplication in research and this can be achieved by setting up joint research groups;
2. they should co-operate in publishing books, as was recommended by the participants at the Kinshasa Conference from 20 to 22 August 1975. They should also exchange information for inclusion in their respective newsletters;
3. the Executive Committee of CODESRIA, meeting at Kinshasa in 1974, decided to hand over the CODESRIA data bank to CERDAS and to entrust the latter with the work of documentation hitherto undertaken by CODESRIA. CODESRIA will have transferred the necessary information to CERDAS by the end of 1975;
4. Professor Bongoy, Acting Director of CERDAS, attended as an observer the CODESRIA meeting held in Kinshasa in 1974. It was suggested that the Director of CERDAS should regularly attend CODESRIA Executive Committee meetings as an observer and that the Executive Secretary of CODESRIA should have the status of observer at CERDAS Governing Board meetings".

In brief, we believe CERDAS has a significant rôle to play in promoting the social sciences in Africa. It will succeed better in this if relations with CODESRIA continue to be as good as they are at present or even improve, and if Unesco, the African States and other financial backers put adequate means at its disposal for research, documentation and the necessary contacts.

Section 3.2. Encouragement should be given to co-operation between African research workers and organizations and those of industrialized countries. The following should nevertheless be clearly defined from the outset:

the general framework into which this co-operation should fall;
the advantages each partner can normally expect to obtain from this co-operation; and
the expenses to be borne by each partner.

Furthermore, once a subject has been properly

defined and stripped to its essentials, the way in which the research is to be carried out must also be specified as well as how the results are to be used and stored, etc. If such preliminary details are not settled there is a risk of falling into the scientific neo-colonialism so strongly resented and abhorred by many governments of underdeveloped countries. Such resentment could be an obstacle to increased communication between rich and poor countries.

One suitable way of encouraging co-operation between industrial countries and African States belonging to CERDAS would be to strengthen the authority and increase the efficiency and influence of CERDAS, thanks to which contacts could be greatly facilitated. This brings us to the fourth and last point.

SECTION 4 - RECOMMENDATIONS

Among the many possible recommendations which might be made, we shall mention the following:

(a) the giving of financial, material and logistic support to the efforts and activities of CERDAS, CODESRIA and several other national social science research organizations;

(b) an increase in the number of symposia, seminars and other meetings between various African and non-African research institutes. Such meetings could take place either under the auspices of Unesco or as joint Unesco-CERDAS undertakings;

(c) research workers from different backgrounds should be encouraged to give their opinions on subjects which they consider of priority importance and, while attempts should be made to harmonize and co-ordinate research work (this might be undertaken by CERDAS, CODESRIA or Unesco), subjects should not be imposed on research workers. Each researcher must at all costs identify himself in one way or another with the subject of his research and take both a personal and scientific interest in it;

(d) the main objective to be pursued seems to be to encourage the social sciences (particularly in Africa) with a view to making them better able to solve the problems arising in human society. In this connexion, the peculiarities and specific features of each human society must be respected and taken into account. Consequently, no recommendation regarding objectives should be made in general, vague terms but should rather be specific and deal with a well-defined subject. What we might reiterate here is that the research subjects chosen must be directed towards solving specific problems in a given society;

(e) Unesco can play a leading part, notably by continuing to organize various symposia and seminars, by making funds available to co-ordinating organizations, and so on. We would like to see Unesco strive to make the social sciences really international and not always continue to give precedence to the same organizations in the same developed countries. Without the contribution of the social sciences in Africa and Asia, it cannot be claimed that social science has been successfully developed nor that co-operation in the social sciences has been speeded up at world level.

CHAPTER 5

Social Science Co-operation in the Arab Region
by
Ahmad M. Khalifa
Director
Centre for Social Science Research
and Documentation for the Arab Region, Cairo

I.   Investigating the question of social science research in the Arab region and how developed it is, in one of the less developed regions of the world should be, in our view, preceded by a prior inquiry into how social science research itself is related to social conditions of any society. Conditions of research are shaped to a great extent by the social conditions rather than by the intrinsic research needs.

Even on the international plane, the state of social science research and the social sciences in general reflects honestly the world situation; power and weakness, wealth and need, division, disagreement, hostility. It reflects too the abyss dividing the world into the developed and the underdeveloped.

I therefore intend to deal with our present subject in two sections: the first on the state of society in the region and the second on the state and general features of social science research.

The most striking feature in the less developed countries is, perhaps, mass poverty. There is of course, a wide variation in per capita income in the oil-producing countries, which amounted to approximately $4,000 or $5,000 compared with $50-$60 in some non-oil-producing countries. Poverty was in some or most cases accentuated by over-population where the two formed a vicious circle.

Moreover, a serious lack of industrial growth impeded the absorption of more workers into the labour force. That lack has led to an increase in the sub-integrated communities that existed on the fringes of ever-inflated urban life. Whenever any degree of development has been achieved, including a growth in GDP, it had not been accompanied by an increase in the level of living for the majority of the lower-income groups.

Of course, the situation characterized by continuing maldistribution of income, unemployment, injustice in regional development and insufficient emphasis on minimum nutritional requirements, poor education, poor training in skills and inadequate health services had worsened as a result of inflation.

It was often maintained that many developing countries were characterized by their "dual structure". The colonial and feudal eras had left a legacy in which it was almost ritualistic to take from the "have-nots" to give to the "haves". The economy and the precarious social services were geared to that end.

The dichotomy between the rural (or bush or desert) and urban environments had sharply divided the social structure. The people's capacity to adapt was so restricted that they were unable to follow the ever-increasing need for change, making any attempt at development extremely difficult.

Persistence of such a distorted socio-economic structure could turn the developmental process into a spontaneous reproduction of underdevelopment. A development strategy based on a large income disparity and a considerable degree of deprivation is a serious obstacle to innovation and prevented nations from realizing their full potential.

Education depersonalized the few who obtained it and created a minority of élite, alienated from the life of the majority of the people and divorced from the real needs of society. After independence, the members of the élite came to power. Although some of them had led the struggle for independence, because the movement was without a rich social content and was not the result of the rise of new productive forces, the élite, ill-equipped to raise the consciousness of their people and foment constructive enthusiasm, settled for maintaining its own privileges.

Some economists, by stressing capital as the key to economic development, ignored the human potential latent in the huge masses once they were mobilized and given an opportunity to deploy their talents politically, economically and socially. In order to inspire the unused human potentialities, it was necessary to abolish all forms of exploitation and enable everyone to enjoy the fruits of equal opportunity. That suggests an inseparable link between development and basic human rights.

Young people, being more liberated from vested interests, were the first to sense disparities and injustice, but they were also the first to be alienated. Since, however, they constitute the bulk of the population in the less developed countries, they should be expected instead to be the striking force in the development process. If youth is not a social class by itself, youth is becoming a force, a labour and a political force, a pressure group, judging by what took place in recent years in various advanced countries. Therefore, whenever we speak of developing youth potential we should think of involvement of youth in development and furthermore, we should not lose sight of the most vital implication: involvement of youth in public life and politics.

Among the young people of the world, in affluent countries as well as in the non-privileged, there exists, at least one element in common: idealism and the search, more or less conscious, for freedom from exploitation and manipulation in all their forms; in short a yearning for honesty, integrity and self-determination. Authoritarianism is still, regretfully, felt throughout the whole world. We might be tempted into more optimistic thinking when we see that the world has almost got rid of the old forms of absolutism. The fact is that the old masks have fallen but new masks are hung hiding the same old face.

In the less developed countries, the case is as simple as this: young people do not take sufficient part in development because they themselves live in a situation of insufficient development, if any.

Speaking of development and human rights, we are reminded of politics being the key to change. Political machinery should, if possible, be devised to assume responsibility for effective socio-economic development. The developing countries were above all in need of political integrity and clarity of mind to undertake basic reforms that could bring greater equality of opportunity and ensure the enjoyment of human rights. In many developing countries, power-hungry governments were perpetuating the state of inequality.

The crucial problem arose: should it always be a matter of a capitalist system of development or could perhaps another form of development be found? What development system was more suited to the backward economies?

We are faced here with a shortcoming of science. Social sciences do not create values nor philosophies, in other words, absolute ends that all other purposes should serve; science and research only strive to co-ordinate means and purposes and help achieve what is needed to fulfil these absolute ends.

Using a metaphor, if development is the train-the rails should be constructed pointing to a certain destination. Where the rails should lead is not a scientific matter; rather, it is a political decision based on value-choice. In this respect, any blurred vision would not help and could cause waste and suffering.

Generally speaking, however, during the past two decades changes in the relationship between the government and the private sector were introduced in a number of countries from developing areas. There was a trend towards an increase in the economic rôle of the public sector, including an increase in nationalization and public ownership of some industries, utilities and financial institutions, and an expansion and diversification of public investment.

Most countries have introduced planning or changed their approach to planning since 1950. In the early 1960s the scope of planning broadened as governments increasingly became involved in determining economic growth targets, guiding the development of productive capacity and infrastructure, allocating resources, curtailing inflation and maintaining economic stability. A common aim was to attain a greater degree of economic independence through greater self-sufficiency and by reducing the constraints of national development resulting from foreign influences and fluctuations in international markets. By the late 1960s, the development plans of several countries broadened in scope to incorporate social as well as economic goals in order to achieve structural change and greater social equality.

Structural changes which might be well suited to one country might not necessarily be advisable in another. For instance, land reform and redistribution might not be desirable in a country where land was abundant and manpower scarce. Similarly, nationalization might not be the best course of action for a country with only a small number of qualified personnel. While underdevelopment is a general phenomenon, its characteristics differ from country to country, and the exact nature of structural changes need to be determined in the light of local circumstances.

Any attempt at structural change requires political will, and it is an unfortunate fact that the régimes of many countries most in need of such change are reluctant to undertake reforms because of the threat which they might pose to the status quo. Another unfortunate fact is that many of the advanced countries are not genuinely concerned with the cause of development in the world at large.

The developing countries often regard that the prospects for their social reforms are severely limited by the structure of the international community as a whole. The current gap between the developed and the underdeveloped countries has become unbearable to both. Over-development is not conceivable without over-exploitation. The developed countries, for their over-accelerated growth, abused energy resources which they obtained at very low prices, thereby shattering the economic well-being of the whole world. It is not surprising then that the gap between countries is widening. The oneness of the world can no longer be overlooked or exploitation tolerated.

All efforts towards development in the less developed countries will be, however, a failure unless there is a will to develop inside the country itself. The gaps in cultural and income levels, which are interrelated, must be closed, at least in part, if the development is to take place.

The economic factors in the developmental process are most relevant and highly significant but no real development could be achieved by economic considerations alone. In order to achieve change, society has to break away from traditional patterns of thought, motivation and behaviour. Development requires a radical change in attitudes. The will to develop requires a capacity to change, and that in turn calls for a certain social atmosphere. The social capacity to adjust and adapt requires a broad social basis that was educated and motivated. Economic phenomena are in fact intertwined with social phenomena, because they are socially conditioned and have social implications. Therefore, planning for development is the same as planning for social change.

In most developing countries of the region there is still a persistence of traditional patterns of thought, especially regarding the status of women. There are many factors which affect the social and economic status of women, especially education and participation in the labour force. Women can contribute to development only through work, and that requires an expansion of education for girls. In this region, in the previous 20 years, the number of girls receiving education increased, but the rate of illiteracy is still too high. The possibility of independent gainful employment for women has decreased the dependence of a wife on her husband and increased her bargaining power within the family unit. In the rural areas, women did the bulk of the routine task, yet received no wages, such work was simply indicative of the low status of women in general. However, if a man is willing to have a working partner he must also to some extent accept the greater demands by the woman to be free from the traditional patterns of labour. The creation of new job opportunities for women therefore went further towards freeing them from male domination than did any bright argument. In the developing countries, however, the employment of women is still regarded as a temporary and exceptional phenomenon and it is thus difficult to regard women as a social force. Largely because of socio-cultural pressures, women fail to share in and identify with social activities. Under the letter of the law, they enjoy political, social and economic rights and the highest government posts are open to them. But full attainment of their rights involves social acceptance, which is contingent upon the degree of maturity and consciousness of both men and women.

In recent research projects correlation has been noted between the status of women and the fertility: the lower the status, the higher the fertility rate. The status of women therefore has implications for national development, especially in terms of fertility differential and it is logical to assume that a woman's attitude is of the utmost importance for fertility rates and any policy of population control.

In one sense, the purpose of development is to change the individual's view of himself and his relationship with others and society. The image of woman should be changed, not only in the eyes of society, but primarily in her own eyes.

II. Needless to say, scientific data, facts, and methods are needed to help solve the problems of development. Social scientists are called upon to carry out their tasks. The question is, however, whether social sciences have failed or not in serving the cause of development in our part of the world?

As we have tried to point out, the social sciences are greatly dependent on society and consequently, the explanation of the crisis is to be sought in the examination of the social conditions in which the social sciences have developed.

National development is a process in which every society should have its own formula corresponding to its particular characteristics. If this is the case, it becomes imperative to approach the development process in our less developed world with the scientific frame of mind and armory conceived and adapted accordingly. Transplantation gets us nowhere. On the other hand, the total repudiation of all that is not indigenous constitutes the other deadly sin of xenophobia.

Social scientists should always bear in mind that the social sciences, unlike exact sciences, cannot be divorced from subjective factors.

We, therefore, cannot be mainly concerned with the epistemological and methodological aspects of the disciplines to the point of considering the present crisis or failure to be symptomatic of the epistemological incertitudes of social sciences.

The question we should ask ourselves should be: are we providing our society with the "scientific" outputs - let us not worry right now about the quality - that our society needs?

Understandably enough, sociology, the anthropology of advanced and civilized societies, is poorly represented in the less developed countries. On the other hand, anthropology, whether an illegitimate of colonialism or a legitimate child of the enlightenment, long prevailed and was a fertile ground for the development of the European "civilizing mission" which became so pervasive during the nineteenth century, and which in fact was the rationalization of more mundane things such as economic plunder, political imposition and other inhuman practices.

After World War II European colonial empires underwent a major crisis which was prompted by severe challenges. The people of the Third World struggled and won independence in the fifties and sixties. The rupture in political and administrative structures jolted the social sciences very badly. Anthropology which hitherto had treated "tribal" societies as static or in "equilibrium" found itself having to explain a number of phenomena which had not been anticipated by its theory. American urban sociology and techniques proved handy to those who were involved in urban studies. More important than that was the predominance of Parsonian variables and Mertonian "rôle theory" in studies of "social change". In the best American spirit "rôle differentiation" and increased individualism became indices of modernity, not a mark of capitalism which was otherwise taken for granted.

The spread of Westernization at the turn of the nineteenth century into many aspects of Egyptian life, to take the example of Egypt, especially in education, economy and legislation, stimulated the translation and writing of several works dealing with social issues which supported or condemned the new changes. The core issue was whether the new changes contradicted the principles and the teachings of Islam or whether Islam as a way of life could accommodate these modern ideas. In this respect, the works and writings of Mohamed Abdu and Kasem Amin, who vigorously supported the new changes, had far-reaching effects. The latter, Kasem Amin, published three fundamental books which are still regarded as important references for social scientists.

Social scientific works by Egyptians began to appear after the establishment of the privately-owned National University in 1908, when students were sent on missions abroad to further their graduate studies. Some of the sociological works in the thirties, reflected the emergence of sociological studies based on field research or data from secondary sources as is evident from the early M. A. sociology theses presented to the Egyptian University.

In spite of these Western influences, a significant factor that accounts for the development of some sort of autonomous sociology in the Arab region is what might be called the Arabic cultural and intellectual heritage which contains many sociological observations on human behaviour.

This heritage includes, among other things, the works of Ibn Khaldun (1332-1406 A. D.) who is regarded by many Western sociologists as one of the important forerunners in the field of sociology. Ibn Khaldun helped the development of sociology in the region by reminding us that sociology is not a foreign commodity imported from the West but is part of the Arab culture, and that they should be proud of it. Many of his theories are sometimes considered still more pertinent and in many ways more appropriate to understanding the social questions and the problems of Arabic societies than the theories of many Western writers who write about the Arab world.

If we take the case of the present generation of our social scientists a great number of whom trained abroad, we will witness a paradox. The overwhelming majority of their dissertations deal with the Arab world in general. Their later works - once back home - do not.

The concern of the authors of these dissertations and theses could be explained by a number of factors. While these authors were studying abroad they observed and felt the deep concern of the sociologists in their universities with their own societies, and the tremendous amount of time, energy and devotion they gave to their problems. They too, witnessed a tremendous amount of interest and involvement in comparative sociology especially the sociology of underdeveloped countries which undoubtedly encouraged them to focus their dissertations on their own countries. Besides, it was much easier for them to write about their own country than to write about a foreign country since they had both the language and the first-hand information of their own societies.

Most of their writings at home, however, show a very different emphasis and orientation. Unlike their dissertations, most of their writings are concerned with general sociology and its subfields. The reason could be that they, upon their return, are pressed to publish books in sociology to fill the rather empty library in Arabic in this field. Besides, writing books on sociology and its fields, seemed easier than doing original research which needs a good deal of energy and patience.

It should be added that quite a number of Western governments interested in knowing more about our social life for political purposes encourage research projects in the domain of the social sciences. Every year, hundreds of Ph. D. students, as well as professors on sabbatical, receive grants to conduct social research in the Middle East and other developing countries.

At present, there is no question about the strong influences of Western sociology on the minds of social scientists in our region. A marked trend, however, geared to indigenization began to be felt in the last decade. In our view this could be attributed to two main reasons: the institutionalization of social science research and the militant sociology which recently made its apparition in the West.

The recent years have witnessed transformations consequent upon the contending movement, which have challenged and called in question the traditional sociology in its ensemble.

The promotion of the contending sociology has brought in its trail a number of new sociological instruments for investigation. One of them is the sociology of sociology. The penetration of the political and social militant spirit among sociologists has changed the trends of development and the contemporary sense of sociology. It can be that it is not the sociologist who has become a militant but the militant who has become a sociologist. A profound cause of the crisis in sociology is to be found in the very fundamental contradictions of society. Despite anthropology, sociology, economics, political science, etc., the peoples of the Third World seem to have made their choice according to their vested interests and not according to some contrived professional code.

In Egypt and in the region as a whole up to the middle of the 1950s, the bulk of sociological and social anthropological studies represented numerous fragmented, embryonic pieces of research conducted or directed by a single researcher, who was either from abroad or trained abroad.

With the establishment of social science research centres in the fifties, the National Centre for Social and Criminological Research in 1956, as well as several other smaller centres and research institutes, research became institutionalized. These centres were able to appoint or gather under their auspices research teams of qualified specialists and trained research assistants to collaborate on investigating specific problems of mutual interest. The centres also succeeded, to a large extent, in obtaining the necessary funds and the needed facilities and equipment to conduct large-scale research operations.

The advantages incurred from this institutionalization of research in the 1950s should not be taken to imply that the problems and obstacles of conducting research in Egypt have been solved. Some of the old problems still remain while several new ones have emerged.

It seems quite obvious that no other country than Egypt within the Arab region can offer the same amount of opportunities for training and research in the social sciences and some of the related sciences. The number of students and people involved in various research projects is, consequently, higher than in any other country within the area. A recently issued bibliography of works by contemporary sociologists in Egypt (having obtained their Ph.D. or M.A. degree before 1972) comprises no less than 83 names and 1,036 titles, 964 of which are in Arabic and 72 in English. In order to give some evidence of the intensity of research in social sciences carried out in some other Arab countries with a relatively high university level, it may be mentioned here that a list of publications by Iraqi sociologists, anthropologists and criminologists does not include more than 18 names and 50 titles, whereas the Lebanese "Institut

des Sciences Sociales" has published the results of 16 research projects undertaken during the period 1969-1974, 25 other research results remaining unpublished, and the American University of Beirut can present a list of 26 M.A. theses in sociology and anthropology covering the period 1955-1973.

Egypt is probably the only country within the Arab world where adequate training in sociology and other social sciences is provided by five national universities; the full-time teaching staff concerned with sociology at these universities amounts today to over one hundred. A serious interest in and support of sociology is shown by authorities, which has resulted in social sciences and social work being regarded as intermingled fields. In Egypt, more than in any other Arab country, efforts have long been made to incorporate social sciences into the scheme of development and welfare.

The contribution of the National Centre for Social and Criminological Research in Egypt remains to be accurately assessed and evaluated now that the Centre has completed twenty years of its existence. It could be said, however, that it has left a clear impact on the state of social sciences in the area. It has helped in many respects:

- Institutionalization of social sciences research in Egypt.
- Ignition of interest in other Arab States and help in the creation of research bodies.
- Producing a huge cadre in the universities, in Egypt and outside Egypt, and other research institutes.
- Compilation of basic surveys.
- Creation, among the general public and planners and policy-makers of an appreciation of the scientific data at the basis of development policies.

In conclusion, the question asked earlier in this paper: Have social sciences failed in serving the cause of development in our part of the world? could be answered with another question: Has the necessary fermentation taken place yet or should we give it some more time?

Maybe we should. Our society is in a state of turmoil and a soul-searching process is well on: are we producing the type of data or using methodology that best fits our own developmental needs?

WORKS CONSULTED

Al-Qazzaz, A. Notes on the State of Sociology in Iraq. Berkeley, 1974. (Unpublished)

Khalifa & Khalifa. Status of Women in Relation to Fertility and Family Planning in Egypt, NCSCR, Cairo, 1973.

Mafeje, A. The Problem of Anthropology in Perspective. The Hague, 1975. (Unpublished)

Natansohn, I. The crisis in sociology and the development of a contending trend. The Social Future (Bucharest). Special Issue for the 8th World Congress of Sociology in Toronto, 1974.

Saafan, H.S. (moogaz Fi Tarikh Elm El-Igtima Fi Masr). A Concise History of Sociology in Egypt, Cairo, El Magliss El Alla Lilfonoon Wal Adab, Cairo, 1970.

CHAPTER 6

Social Science Co-operation in Europe

by
Adam Schaff

President, European Co-ordination Centre for
Research and Documentation in Social Sciences, Vienna

1. THE HISTORY, FUNCTIONS AND ORGANIZATION OF THE CENTRE

The European Co-ordination Centre for Research and Documentation in Social Sciences (hereafter called "the Centre") was called into being following a unanimous vote by the Unesco General Conference in 1962.

Vienna became the seat of that new European organization. The choice of Austria was motivated by that country's neutrality and location in the centre of Europe. A special rôle in making Vienna the seat of the Centre was played by the Austrian Government, who not only gave the organizers its full support but also comprised the new institution in its ambitious and consistent policy of turning Vienna into a place of international meetings and a seat of international organizations.

The organization of the Centre was entrusted by Unesco to the International Social Science Council; the statute of the Centre makes it an autonomous agency of that Council. Following the Unesco resolution all European countries are entitled to participate in the Centre's activities and are supposed to subsidize them.

When formed, the Centre had two principal tasks to perform:

(i) to set up a European platform for co-operation by social scientists (in the broad sense of the term) in international comparative studies; that platform was supposed first of all to promote co-operation between scholars from socialist and capitalist countries;

(ii) to work out the methodology and research techniques of international comparative studies in the social sciences.

The Centre was set up as a co-ordinating agency, and not as a research institute. Research was to be conducted by national research teams, and the Centre was merely to co-ordinate it. This has obviously affected its structure and organization.

The Centre is governed by the Board of Directors, appointed by the International Council of Social Science on the basis of the equal participation of scholars from European socialist and capitalist countries (it has 16 members at present). The directors choose one of them to be the Board's chairman, who runs the Centre in the periods between the sessions of the Board; his term of office is three years.

The Board of Directors makes decisions on the choice of research projects, appoints project leaders, supervises research work and makes decisions in budgetary matters.

Organizing and co-ordinating work is being done by the Scientific Secretariat (headed by a director), which is assisted by the Technical Secretariat. The former includes assistant professors delegated to the Centre by their mother organizations, whether scientific or governmental, and paid by them; when delegated to the Scientific Secretariat, its members have to stay in Vienna (on the average for a period of three years); each of them has to co-ordinate one or two research projects. The Centre at present has ten such scientific secretaries, including the Secretariat's director, who is delegated to the Centre on the same basis.

The Centre has so far undertaken 20 international research projects in the various spheres of social science, such as: time budgets, juvenile delinquency; Third World students in Europe; backward regions in advanced countries; the future of the rural areas in advanced countries; automation and industrial workers; comparative forms of aid to the developing countries; capacity of absorption of external aid by the developing countries and problems of transfer of technology; cost of urban growth; the image of the world of the year 2000; and so forth.

The Centre's budget (including research work, international meetings, publications, etc.) - which now amounts to ca. US $250,000 in exchangeable currencies and ca. US $125,000 in non-exchangeable currencies - is covered by voluntary subsidies from European governments and other institutions. The number of participant countries has recently risen to 22, six of which are socialist countries.

Those readers who would be interested in the organization and functioning of the Centre in greater detail must be referred to a paper dedicated to the ten years of its activity[1]. What follows will deal mainly with political and research problems as reflected in the experience accumulated by the Centre.

2. THE POLITICAL ASPECTS OF THE CENTRE'S ACTIVITY

The history, organization and activity of the Centre being outlined above, we now have to explain the guiding principles and objectives of that institution, and to draw general conclusions from its experience, conclusions applicable to international cooperation in the sphere of social science.

As has been mentioned above, the initiators and organizers of the Centre were guided by two clear objectives which, organically interconnected as they are, should rather be presented separately. One objective was political, and the other scientific in nature.

Let us begin with discussing the political objective, because only by doing so can we comprehend both the origin of that institution and its subsequent development, both its specific problems and the stimuli which helped that development.

In order clearly to see the political objective which was the underlying idea of the Centre we have to comprehend in detail the political context of the period which saw the birth of the initiative for setting up the Centre under consideration. It was the year 1962, the year which saw the beginning of the policy of peaceful coexistence. It is not our task to explain here the assumptions and basic ideas of that policy. Suffice it to say that the said policy marked an endeavour to put an end to the cold war, and hence an endeavour to bring closer countries with different socio-political systems, or, to put it plainly, socialist and capitalist countries. The policy of coexistence was based on two principles: (a) renunciation of the use of force in international relations, which reduced the rivalry between the two systems to a peaceful competition, among other things in the sphere of ideology; (b) the explicit statement, at least on the part of the socialist countries, that the principle of coexistence does not apply to ideology. This meant that the ideological struggle between the two systems could, and even had to be continued if, while eliminating the use of force from international relations, ideology was considered to be one of the favourable battlefields for the rival socio-political systems, even though these do not engage in any armed conflict.

Let us leave aside the problem of meaning of such basic terms connected with that idea, such as coexistence, ideology, ideological coexistence, etc., which would open vast grounds for verbal misunderstandings. While one started from assumptions burdened with obscurities, verbal controversies and misunderstandings, one saw clearly that international politics, especially in the sphere of relations between the East and the West (in the somewhat conventional, political and not geographical, sense of these terms) was entering a stage of détente and tentative rapprochements. That fact, of course, favoured rapprochements in other fields too, including that of science and research. Otherwise any initiative to start joint comparative studies in social science in both Eastern and Western Europe would not only be incomprehensible, but would have to be dismissed as utterly unrealistic. Under the new conditions, however, that initiative became at least potentially realistic.

Yet the situation at that time was by no means clear, and hence the scepticism voiced from various quarters was not groundless. For while the policy of peaceful coexistence implied a détente and rapprochements between countries which belonged to the different socio-political systems in Europe, it was being emphasized explicitly that that did not apply to all the spheres of social life, that ideological issues were not covered by the policy of coexistence and that in that sphere no rapprochement was to be expected. On the contrary, the conflict in that field would intensify. And it is to be borne in mind that the social sciences are ideological in nature.

In that complex situation, which in a sense was marked by inner contradictions, it was the political argument which had the upper hand: the trend toward the détente and rapprochement prevailed. Or it would perhaps be more realistic to say that no one was willing to incur the odium of openly attacking the idea of coexistence, an idea so attractive to public opinion. The vote on the setting up of the Centre, taken at the Unesco General Conference in 1962, was unanimous: the Centre was to become a meeting ground for cooperation between social scientists from European countries with different socio-political systems. That unanimity was significant but, to be objective, it should be noted that the vote was unanimous because abstentions are disregarded, and - which is much more difficult to assess - it may be assumed that some, and possibly many, votes were for the proposal only because the very idea of the Centre was thought unrealistic and hence doomed to failure.

At that time it was, in fact, difficult to believe that the project would succeed in view of the numerous real obstacles.

First, the genuine ideological division of Europe, at that time vigorously reinforced by the apprehensions on both sides of the barrier that

----

(1) cf. Riccardo Petrella, Adam Schaff, Une expérience de coopération européenne dans les sciences sociales. Dix ans d'activité du Centre. 1963-1973. Centre Européen, 1973.

decreased tension, a weakened sense of danger and less isolation could weaken the unity in the conflict with the other side. It could accordingly be expected that any proposal for co-operation in the touchy sphere of ideology would be torpedoed in order not to make the impression that existing divisions were at least partially artificial. The very idea of the Centre, which was to stimulate and organize international co-operation precisely in that field, was to abolish a taboo. It was obvious that, should the experiment succeed, it would be a precedent whose significance would go far beyond the domain of science and research and would result in a reformulation of the issue of ideological barriers in other spheres of social life. That was clear to all, and even the organizers of the Centre were not sure of success. And the difference between the various forms of scepticism was rather such that the "enthusiasts" thought that the experiment might succeed, whereas representatives of political "common sense" were convinced that it would fail.

This resulted in the second objective obstacle: there were neither sufficient financial means nor sufficient staff to cope with at least some of the tasks with which the new Centre was bountifully entrusted.

Denial of means to an organization which was certainly doomed to failure was probably a manifestation of the "common sense" mentioned above. Now that one looks back already rich with the experience acquired later, one must say that when the Centre started its triumphant march with only one scientific and one technical secretary, it was only the utter ignorance of the obstacles to be encountered on the way which made that folly possible.

Thirdly, the pioneering nature of the research tasks which the Centre had to carry out also was a serious obstacle. At that time international, multilateral and, to make the matter even more complicated, interdisciplinary comparative studies in the sphere of social science were still in a nascent stage, and that even as theoretical considerations rather than actual research work. And when it comes to comparative studies, in which countries belonging to different socio-political systems in Europe were supposed to participate on the basis of parity, they were still non-existent; there had even never been any endeavour to organize them, and it was also by no means clear whether they would be possible at all in view of differences in theoretical and methodological approaches to various issues in the socialist countries in Eastern Europe and in the capitalist ones in Western Europe.

Considering these difficulties, whose list as given above was far from being complete, one could conclude that the undertaking was Utopian in nature, and the setting up of the Centre was in fact a symbolic gesture not supposed to have any practical consequences whatever. And yet things have turned otherwise. Despite all the initial problems, despite the ominous obstacle which was the political crisis in some European countries in 1968, and which was a strong blow against the still nascent activity of the Centre, the institution has not only withstood the impact of outward complications but has won universal European acceptance and succeeded - when the Unesco subventions were terminated - in raising itself the necessary funds in the form of voluntary contributions by European countries.

How has it come to that? What were the factors which have turned what had seemed a Utopian dream into a fact deeply rooted in European realities?

As has been said earlier, the success was based on the general atmosphere of international détente due to the policy of peaceful coexistence.

The rôle of two institutions, Unesco and the International Social Science Council, must be emphasized since without their support the idea of setting up the Centre would have never been born.

An important rôle in the Centre's development has been played by the warm response on the part of social scientists in Europe. If one considers the fact that the Centre has never paid for research, which was due not only to its restricted means but also to the principle that co-operation with the Centre must be based on goodwill; that at one time co-operation within the research projects sponsored by the Centre could seem risky as to the final effects of the work engaged in them because it was not certain that the Centre would survive for several years; and that the participants in a research project had to spend five years on it on the average, then the only explanation is that the Centre's activity was gaining increasing support on the part of European social scientists, and above all that those scientists had realized the importance of comparative studies in general, and these conducted simultaneously in countries with different socio-political systems in particular. That support, or even enthusiasm, on the part of social scientists in Europe, to a European platform of joint research was decisive for the development of the Centre and for the overcoming of the difficulties it encountered.

It is also necessary to emphasize the rôle and achievements of the group of enthusiasts on the Board of Directors and in the Scientific Secretariat; their vigour and hard work have been the immediate source of the success the Centre has attained.

But while we fully appreciate the importance of the vigour and hard work of those people for the Centre's success, one has above all to stress the tactics deliberately adopted by the organizers of the Centre in planning its structure and functioning. In my opinion it was that tactic which made the Centre overcome the numerous obstacles resulting from the differences in the political and ideological systems of the participant countries. Its experience can, and should, serve as a model in promoting similar initiatives in international co-operation.

From the very beginning the functioning of

the Centre has been based on the rigorous principle of strict equilibrium of influences of the East and the West. The point was trivial: to avoid suspicion, and possibility, of the political or ideological domination of the Centre by one side. Hence the Board of Directors (whose number was growing) was based on the principle that the number of its members from one side must strictly correspond to that from the other: the Board had at first 5 + 5, and now 8 + 8 members. Voting in the Board has always been on the unanimity principle (even though that is not required by the statute), so that the opposition on the part of any member has in fact been treated as a veto in order to avoid conflicts. Each research project has two co-directors, one from each side. Research (covered by a given project) is always conducted in countries in both parts of Europe; comparative studies confined to one part of Europe are not permitted. For all the difficulties connected with the financing of the stay in Vienna of those members of the Scientific Secretariat who come from the socialist countries efforts have been made (recently crowned with success owing to Unesco assistance) to reach full equilibrium on that point too. Was that all necessary? Have there ever been conflicts of this kind? No, the 12 years in the history of the Centre have not witnessed any such conflict, and co-operation has been perfect. But it has perhaps been so just because the possible sources of such conflicts have been eliminated (this applies above all to suspicions of conditions that would favour ideological domination by a single group), and that is why such a pedantic principle of equilibrium was required, or has at least proved useful in practice.

The said principle has been observed all the time: the point was to preserve the international character of the Centre, to prevent it from becoming a national institution as a result of its being dominated by the staff recruited from one country. The organizers of the Centre have drawn conclusions from the history of many scientific institutions which, while called into being as international ones, later transformed themselves into national ones just to cease to exist. The danger was seen in making apparently sound decisions, with economies, etc., in view, to rely out of proportion on the local staff which necessarily results in a gradual change of the nature of a given international agency.

The Centre was deliberately made to follow a different course, even though this meant difficulties and privations. As in the case of the principle of not financing the work done by national research teams in order to be sure that their co-operation with the Centre is dictated exclusively by their interest in a given project and in international co-operation as such, the adoption of the principle that research workers must be delegated by their mother institutions which have to pay them had the same end in view. The point was to make European countries and institutions committed to

European scientific co-operation. It was not an easy course to follow. I would even say that inducing the countries and institutions concerned to contribute financially to the Centre (and to cover all its expenses now that the Unesco subsidies have expired) was a calvary to the Centre's managers, but it certainly was an effective policy if we consider the Centre's objectives.

The Centre has fairly soon achieved success when it comes to the political goals set themselves by the organizers. First, the Centre has won green light for its activity throughout Europe. For instance, the Centre organized a conference on the new research project on "The future of rural communities in Europe", held in Warsaw in 1971 and attended by representatives of 14 European countries, namely seven East European and seven West European ones. It is to be noted that the latter included Spain and Portugal, even though at that time these did not have diplomatic relations with Poland. So far over 250 research institutes from nearly all European and numerous non-European countries have co-operated with the Centre. This fact alone testifies to the all-European character of the Centre.

The success the Centre has had during the past 12 years has a number of practical consequences. They prove that co-operation of social scientists from countries with different socio-political systems and joint comparative studies are possible and that they do not encounter any serious obstacles if they are prepared and conducted in a proper way.

The example of the Centre and its success have stimulated other organizations and institutions to act, which has largely expanded international co-operation in social science. The results of comparative studies sponsored by the Centre have shown that such studies are not only important from the theoretical point of view, but also have considerable practical and political significance. Finally, in the light of the present day trend for European integration, in particular following the Conference on Security and Co-operation in Europe, we have to expect the growth of European non-governmental organizations also in the field of science and culture. The experience of the Centre may help stimulate further activity in that field.

3. THE SCIENTIFIC ASPECT OF
    THE CENTRE'S ACTIVITY

Let us now discuss the second, scientific, objective which the organizers of the Centre had in view.

As mentioned earlier, international comparative studies in social science were still in a nucleus stage at the time the Centre was being organized, and the tasks set the Centre in that sphere were of a pioneering nature. This applies in particular to comparative studies covering both socialist and capitalist countries, as it involves additional difficulties resulting from different theoretical and methodological approaches to social research. That sphere certainly was an unknown land, and the newly organized Centre was faced with novel tasks.

The question about the purpose of the comparative studies undertaken by the Centre can be answered as follows:

First, such studies, as emphasized earlier, were to serve as a platform for co-operation of scholars representing different disciplines and originating from countries with different historical, cultural and socio-political traditions, scholars who represented different schools of thought both when it comes to their strictly scientific opinions and their ideologies.

Secondly, the objective was to acquire better information about various social problems through a systematic accumulation and comparative elaboration of data, intended to bring out the rôle of diverse variables in social development. Research sponsored by the Centre always treats the socio-political system as one of the variables, which means investigating the rôle played in a given case by differences in socio-political systems. It is unnecessary to add that such research has both theoretical and practical importance.

Thirdly, in view of the methodological weakness of comparative studies in social science the point was to make a step forward in the methodology and techniques of such research; this was to be achieved through research conducted within the projects sponsored by the Centre.

Considering the tasks with which the Centre was faced questions about the rôle of the Centre in the choice of the subject-matter of research, in organizing, conducting and co-ordinating such research, and in the final working out and publication of the results obtained had to be answered. Some answers were clear from the very beginning and formed the principles on which the Centre was to operate. Other answers came as a result of later experiences and discussions. In any case, those issues which many a time were discussed in depth by the Board of Directors are now clarified and the resulting answers not only form foundations of our activity but also may be treated as the Centre's contribution to further international co-operation in social science.

The starting point for comments on those issues and on the solutions adopted may take on the form of the fundamental statement that the Centre is not a research institute but an agency which co-ordinates research conducted by national teams of workers, research which it promotes and supervises. The Centre accordingly does not (and neither can nor should) set itself any tasks in the field of its own research work, as it is neither expected to do so nor has the means necessary for such activity. Its proper function is to provide a meeting ground for social scientists who would co-operate on the European scale, and to promote and co-ordinate international comparative studies in social science. In view of the above the Centre, which operates through the intermediary of its Board of Directors and its Scientific Secretariat, has the following tasks to perform:

(i) To select the subject-matter of research, in which it should be guided by the scientific importance of each research, its agreement with the political goals of the Centre and the feasibility. The choise is made by the Board of Directors.

(ii) To organize an international network of research by appointing adequate research teams (mainly in European countries) and to choose the leaders of a given research project on the international scale. This is the task of the Scientific Secretariat, the appointment of the leaders of research projects being a prerogative of the Board of Directors.

(iii) To co-ordinate the national research teams within a given international research project. This prerogative of the Scientific Secretariat covers: (a) organization of the work of the international group of experts who prepare a given research design and its research instruments and set the deadlines; all national groups have to work in accordance with these decisions; (b) co-ordination of the work of such national teams by organizing periodical meetings (to be held once or twice a year) of representatives of the national teams to compare results and possibly to modify the ways in which research is conducted; (c) co-ordination of the work of the editorial committee which prepares the results of the research for publication.

These tasks of the Centre have never provoked any reservations. The Centre accordingly acts as an agency which promotes appropriate international research, organizes and co-ordinates it, and finally publishes the results. But the tacit assumption is that such research is conducted not by the Centre, but by properly selected national research teams, while the scientific aspect of research is in the hands of the scholars themselves, from among whom the leaders of a given research project is chosen.

And what are the functions and tasks of the Centre, its Board of Directors and its Scientific Secretariat when it comes to the scientific guidance of research? While there are no doubts as to the organizational prerogatives of those two bodies (see above), the controversy was over the said scientific guidance.

That controversy resulted from the nature of international research sponsored by the Centre and from the Centre's character.

A given research project is carried out by a sui generis federation of national research teams, which has its research design and research instruments. Each such group is headed by a leader, and the research project as a whole has two co-directors who, together with the leaders of the national teams, form the scientific leadership of the project.

Research work under a given project is organized, co-ordinated and supervised by the Centre's Scientific Secretariat which acts through that scientific secretary who is in charge of that project. He has all the threads in his hands: the relevant correspondence, contacts between the scientific leadership and the national groups, contacts among the national groups, organization of meetings, current supervision, etc. These are organizational and administrative functions, but are they merely that? Obviously not. The scientific secretary is a member of the leadership of a given project, and hence his rôle is a function of two variables: the activeness and effectiveness of the leadership and his own personality as scientist. The history of the research projects sponsored by the Centre has known various relationships between the leadership of a given project and its scientific secretary: in one extreme, the secretary was reduced to the rôle of an organizer only, in the other, he participated to a large extent in providing scientific guidance and in fact shaped the conception of research. Such individual differences cannot, and should not, be regulated in any strict manner, because any such artificial regulation would be swept aside by the course of events. But the issue at stake was the principle, and it was on the principle that the discussion was focused.

The discussions again revealed two extreme standpoints, at various periods taken by various people in view of the problems emerging in specified situations.

One of these extreme standpoints was that the Centre should perform administrative functions only, leaving all scientific guidance to the managers of the project. The Board of Directors would accordingly have just to give its approval in order to support the case with the authorities of the countries concerned, and in addition to that it should provide technical assistance to be handled by the scientific secretary in charge of the project.

The other extreme standpoint was that the Centre should have the scientific guidance of the research projects, thus eliminating in practice the leading rôle of the scholars who are members of the national teams; this would transform the Centre into a research institute whose staff would directly guide research work.

Both extreme standpoints are wrong and have been rejected by the Board of Directors as a result of the experience accumulated by the Centre.

Reflection on the organizational structure and functions of the Centre shows that the Centre cannot be transformed into a large technical secretariat without being deprived of its basic tasks and functions. Practical experience also is against this standpoint. Yes, the history of the Centre has seen very active, and even aggressive, project directors who in fact acted as scientific leaders of a given project. It has also seen quite different cases. But even in those cases in which the director(s) played the dominant rôle in guiding the project it was not correct a priori to eliminate the rôle of the Scientific Secretariat of the Centre. Experience has shown that such trends are detrimental to the projects concerned.

The opposite standpoint is equally wrong. The Scientific Secretariat neither can nor should snatch the scientific guidance of a given project. I would even say that it should be prohibited from doing so. As has been said above, the Centre is not a research institute, and it would be nonsensical to set up one such institute more, which would include the adjective "European" in its name, but would be incomparably weaker than the weakest of all existing national institutes, as its staff would be ridiculously small and quite heterogeneous from the point of view of the specialization of its members. The Centre's tasks are different and consist not in its own research work, but in stimulating and organizing the research conducted by others. From that point of view its organizational tasks and its staff are adequate for its tasks. Neither its director nor its scientific secretaries can claim to know a given problem better than the specialists engaged in research do. But should it even be so they should not replace the specialists, they should not guide a given project for them, since the very sense of the Centre's activity is to make national teams work and co-operate.

To sum up the discussion on the scientific guidance of research projects: the conclusion is that the Centre cannot, and should not, confine itself to organizing and administrative work, but may, and should, participate in the scientific guidance of projects. But, on the other hand, it should not assume exclusive guidance. And what this means in a given case must depend on the conditions under which a given research project is conducted.

The scientific aspect of the Centre's activity is linked with the problem of the standard of the output which is the result of research.

There is no doubt that the attainment of the Centre's principal objective, i.e. providing a meeting ground for co-operation of social scientists on a European scale, is organically connected with a specified standard of the Centre's scholarly output, since otherwise no respectable researcher would risk spending years of work on a project sponsored by the Centre. It was feared at one time that that standard would not be attained under the conditions imposed upon international co-operation by the organizational pattern of the Centre. Today, we can judge the effects on the basis of the several volumes of studies published by the Centre and some 200 papers which are a result of the Centre's activity.

General reflections on the standard of studies that could be attained are to the point if we consider not only the studies published by the Centre but also that which it is possible to achieve in the case of such comparative studies.

Let us repeat what has been said earlier but what is not always grasped properly; the Centre is not a research institute, and it does not undertake its own research work. It does co-ordinate research conducted by national teams and it is its task to stimulate, organize and co-ordinate co-operation among such teams. While it accordingly strives, which is obvious, to ensure the highest possible standard of research undertaken under existing conditions, the Centre depends in that striving on the following factors of which the standard of its scholarly output is a function:

(a) the theoretical and methodological level of a given discipline, with a special consideration of the methodology of comparative international studies;
(b) the level of that discipline in the countries which participate in a given project.

It is common knowledge that empirical studies in social science reveal various shortcomings and are subject to various limitations, which affects the level of the output as a whole. It would be absurd to expect that international comparative studies, burdened with additional difficulties, could overcome the weakness of a given discipline.

This is just trivial. But the differentiation of the level of development of the various disciplines in different countries is much less so. Specialists are fully aware of this differentiation and they are in a position precisely to define the level of development of the social sciences in the various European countries. There are European countries which are advanced in that respect, and there are those in which the level of the development of the social sciences is average or low. And it must be noted that the level of development of those disciplines does not in the least coincide with other indicators of the level of development of those countries, their aims, political importance, etc.

Now the Centre's task is not to select teams from those countries which are advanced as to the level of a given discipline and thereby to assure the highest possible level of the output, but to promote European co-operation. While it may know in advance that the research team of a given European country is weak because the discipline in question is little advanced in that country, the Centre should include a team from the country in research work if it is willing to participate in it. The Centre should do so not only in order to ensure the all-European nature of its activity, but also - which is an important point - to carry out its, as it were, teaching functions, for one of its tasks is to raise the level of social science in Europe. One of the ways in which that goal can be attained is to let weaker research teams be trained in practice by advanced ones. The Centre has done much in this field. In any case it is self-evident what the Centre's options have been, and

should have been, when the Centre was faced with the dilemma outlined above. This seems to be a broader issue, and the Centre's experience to date deserved being considered.

The international character of the comparative studies sponsored by the Centre thus adds one more dimension to the difficulties with which the Centre is faced. Admission of weak research teams as participants in such studies means an extra burden and the deliberate acceptance of a lower standard of research. For all that it has been a correct decision. Does it mean acceptance of a sui generis fatalism in that respect? Is the rôle of the Centre and its scholarly staff reduced in such cases to that of a passive observer?

Certainly not. In such situations the duties of the scientific staff of the Centre increase, and this does not apply to the organizational aspect alone. This is an additional argument against the extreme standpoint of those who would like the Centre to be merely an organizational and technical agency.

But the issue does not boil down to rescue operations, since it also has a much broader and much more important aspect.

One of the tasks with which the Centre has been faced since its very inception was to improve the methodology and research techniques of international comparative studies in social science. Its implementation consisted mainly in properly assisting the various research projects, and that was almost automatically linked with the Centre's routine work, with the accumulation of research experience in the course of its normal functioning. But the Centre has also had, since the very beginning, a more difficult and higher-level task, namely that of methodological metaflection on its own research practice and on the experience accumulated during comparative studies undertaken outside the sphere of the Centre's activity. It is obvious that this required time, above all because of the need to amass data on which general analytical reflection could be based.

The first such undertaking, organized jointly with the Standing Committee on Comparative Studies attached to the International Social Science Council, was the round-table conference on the survey method, held in Budapest in July 1972 and attended by some 40 experts from Europe, the United States and Canada[1]. The debates covered five large-scale international studies carried out during the five years preceding the conference. Thus the point was not to engage in abstract methodological discussions, but to draw conclusions from specified research projects, which certainly was a novel

(1) A book including various reports to the round table is under publication: Cross-national comparative survey research: theory and practice, ed. by A. Szalai and R. Petrella in collaboration with S. Rokkan and E. Scheuch, Oxford, Pergamon Press, 1976.

feature. The discussions will be reflected in an appropriate publication.

This has inaugurated scientific undertakings of a new type, undertakings which the Centre helps organize. It is planned that appropriate conferences should take place once in every two or three years.

Specific proposals concerning co-operation of the European Centre with the co-ordination centres for social sciences in Africa and Latin America

At present, besides the European Centre in Vienna, there are three other such institutions for cross-national social science co-ordination: two in Africa and one in Latin America. Particularly if it were to be under the aegis of Unesco which created all four centres, a programme of mutual co-operation and research would seem advantageous to all.

Although the precise tasks and structure of these four centres may well differ as will the local needs and conditions which they will have to serve, their fundamental aims are the same. Thus, a systematic exchange of ideas and experience must be fruitful for all. In particular, the new centres may find it highly beneficial to be brought into contact with the considerable experience accumulated by the European Centre in its 12 years of existence.

As a first step, the European Centre might be involved in training staff members for the other centres. Such training would involve study of the history, stages of preparation, implementation and analysis of the various research projects which the Vienna Centre has undertaken. This would serve as a good initial guide for scientists newly active in this domain. It would provide a worthwhile grounding in the methods and problems of cross-national comparative research in the social sciences. Staff from our Centre would be prepared to visit the other centres, or alternatively trainees would be welcome in Vienna - although the costs of their stay could not be funded from Vienna Centre sources.

A second possibility for co-operation which goes beyond the simple communication of experience and insights would stem from the launching of common scientific endeavours. These could be of two types: either a repetition of projects already undertaken by the Centre, or the undertaking of new research projects on topics of common social, economic and political interest.

Although any repetition of projects already undertaken by the Vienna Centre would probably require some adaptation to meet the particular circumstances of researchers in different continents, it could well serve as a useful testing ground for the capacities of the new centres. Almost all past projects of the Vienna Centre would seem amenable for such repetition; two present projects might also seem particularly appropriate: "The future of rural communities" and the "Cost of urban growth". As part of this process, one could easily envisage encounters between the European Centre and other social scientists, and these discussions could well pave the way for trans-continental comparative studies undertaken by research teams from the different continents.

There is, without doubt, substantial scope for new common projects. For example, a project on the relationships between donors and recipients of economic aid; or on the socio-economic effects of the transfer of technology. Trans-continental research is already feasible, since the Centre has included amongst its participants such countries as Japan, United States and Mexico. We would be prepared both to develop initiatives and respond to any new ideas of this type. Additionally, it might be possible to use UNDP funds to finance such joint endeavours outside Europe.

The third area for mutual exchange is that of documentation. Although the European Centre has been prevented by lack of funds from undertaking much substantial work in this area, and has refrained from entering it because of Unesco's UNISIST Programme, we may be able to provide or at least facilitate some help to the other centres in this work.

CHAPTER 7

European Co-operation in Development Research, Training and Documentation
The European Association of Development Research and Training Institutes

by
Arne Haselbach

Executive Secretary, European Association
of Development Research and Training Institutes

I. ESTABLISHMENT, OBJECTIVES AND ANTECEDENTS

After more than two years' preparatory work, the European Association of Development Research and Training Institutes (EADI)[1] was founded on 12 September 1975 in Linz, Austria. Initiated by common consent of institutes in all parts of Europe this step towards intensifying and institutionalizing co-operation among institutes and individual researchers working in the field of development is already beginning to show first results.

Less than a year after its establishment, the Association today comprises 100 institutes and 60 individual scientists from 19 European countries. EADI's Secretariat, located in Vienna[2], the Executive Committee[3] and a number of working groups have commenced activities, two issues of the "EADI-Bulletin" have appeared both in French and English and a Report on the Linz Conference of EADI[4] was published.

Objectives

The European Association aims to promote research and training activities in development, as approached through the social sciences and interdisciplinary studies.[5]

EADI shall pursue these aims by promoting contacts and collaboration among its members. At the same time - and equally important - it shall further and facilitate exchanges, working contacts and co-operation between its members on the one hand and regional associations, research and training institutions and researchers in Africa, Asia, Latin America on the other.

The Association will hold itself at the disposal of those institutions and researchers with a view to facilitating their access to sources of information and the instruments of work and research available in Europe.

In order to ensure that this inter-regional co-operation will be useful for the Third World, the constitution of EADI provides for ex officio membership of representatives of the African, Asian and Latin American regional associations in the Executive Committee of EADI.

Historical background

It was on the occasion of a conference devoted to research on social and economic development in April 1973 that a small number of researchers from various European countries got together to discuss possibilities of systematic co-operation between their respective institutes. Since time was short and only a few institutes were represented, those present concentrated on discussing where and when a representative group might be gathered together without undue additional cost. As the Institute of Development Studies at the University of Sussex was at that time planning the "Second National Development Research Conference"[6], it issued invitations to a number of scientists in other European countries to attend the conference and to discuss the usefulness and possible forms of further collaboration among European institutions during a consultation at the end of the conference.

The consultation in East Anglia

The meeting of the University of East Anglia took place on 22 September 1973. It was attended by social scientists from Austria, Belgium, the Federal Republic of Germany, France, the Netherlands, Norway, Poland, Sweden, Switzerland and the United Kingdom. Enrique Oteiza, Executive Secretary of the Latin American Social Science Council, and Poona Wignaraja of the Asian Association of Development Research and Training Institutes reported on experiences of their regional organizations.

From the discussions, and in the light of the experiences of the regional associations in Africa, Asia and Latin America, the adumbrated idea of forming a European association of institutions engaged in research and training on problems of development took on clearer shape. The purpose of such an organization was to be the promotion of exchanges and co-operation among European institutes and the intensification and broadening of relations between institutions in Europe and in the Third World. The association envisaged was to be careful not to lend itself to the creation of over-bureaucratic and costly structures and to avoid any duplication with current activities.

A small committee under the chairmanship of Professor A.A.J. Van Bilsen was charged with conducting soundings and preparations. The necessary contacts having been established the Interdisciplinary Research and Training Centre for Development Co-operation of the University of Ghent issued invitations for the association's first conference which was held in Ghent on 26 and 27 September 1974. That conference agreed on the proposal to found a European Association and charged a considerably enlarged committee with preparing the details for the establishment of the association, scheduled to take place during a further conference, at Linz, in September 1975.

In addition to planning and initiating substantive work of the future association, the Preparatory Committee assigned to the General Conference of 1975 the main theme - "A new international order - economic, social and political implications", and decided to conduct a considerable number of working group sessions in order to test the feasibility of further working groups. An invitation issued by the Vienna Institute for Development, offering to conduct the conference and to bear the expenses, was gratefully accepted and the director of that body charged with organizing the conference.

The 1975 EADI General Conference, Linz, was the highlight of a series of conferences on development research and development strategies(7). In their principal addresses, Mr. Shridath S. Ramphal (Commonwealth Secretary-General), Professor Peter Mandi (Institute for World Economics, Hungarian Academy of Sciences) and Mr. Paul-Marc Henry (President, OECD Development Centre), brilliantly outlined the essential aspects of the main theme. Another major emphasis of the conference was the actual starting of the scientific work of EADI in the various working groups. Proceedings culminated in the Constituent General Assembly of EADI which promulgated the association's constitution, designated Vienna as the seat of the organization and elected the Executive Committee for a period of three years.

II.   MODES AND AREAS OF OPERATION

Less than a year having elapsed since the inception of EADI, it is only natural that this can be but an interim report. If the initiatives here presented are already quite numerous, this is so because EADI is much more a process of intensification of co-operation than an institution; a process that started with the first discussions aiming at its creation; a process in which initiatives are taken, some of which come to fruition whilst others, despite many attempts at reactivation, have to be abandoned; a process the results of which - even up to now - have already proved its usefulness and which has considerable potential for the future.

So far the major part of activities has been devoted to the improvement of the inner-European co-operation. The modes and areas of co-operation with the regional associations of Africa, Asia and Latin America will be discussed in detail in August and September 1976 and could lead to an almost world-wide network of co-operation.

A.   Documentation

Already during the consultation at East Anglia a document submitted by the Sussex Institute of Development Studies, which listed the research projects in the field of development currently being undertaken in the United Kingdom, received the attention of participants. Improvement of documentation via enlarged collaboration was also one of the main agenda items at Ghent. In April 1975 the preparatory committee decided to set up a task force, chaired by Professor C.A.O. van Nieuwenhuijze, then Rector of the Institute of Social Studies, The Hague, charged with examining the problems of information and documentation exchange both among members of the association and between them and the regional associations, and with submitting proposals for improvement.

The Working Group "Documentation and Information" met during the Linz Constituent Assembly and outlined a work programme for the near future. Desiring quick progress in this field the working group decided to meet again in November 1975.

At the invitation of the German Foundation for International Development the group held a workshop in Bonn on 11 and 12 November 1975. Members of the group reported on the state of documentation in their respective countries. They discussed the feasibility of the specific tasks included in the work programme and picked a few for priority attention. In addition the group decided in principle to meet once a year to ensure continuity of its work.

European Register of Ongoing Development Research Projects

It is most important that research in progress should be surveyed and publicized at frequent intervals in order to increase efficiency and prevent possible duplications in European development research. Pioneering efforts were performed in this field by three institutions:

- the OECD Development Centre, which for many years past has included reports about ongoing research projects in its "Liaison-Bulletin";

- the German Foundation for International Development (DSE) with its presentation and documentation, since 1966, in its published series, "Entwicklungsländer-Studien", of current and completed research undertakings on problems of developing countries; and
- the Institute of Development Studies at the University of Sussex, which publishes its "Development Studies - Register of UK-based Ongoing Research" since 1970.

EADI is not proposing to substitute these efforts by a centralized European one. Instead, it is trying to ensure that ongoing research in as many countries as possible will get documented in such a way that interested institutions all over the world would know who is working on which specific issues at any given moment.

Two initiatives have so far been taken towards this end. The University of Antwerp's Centre for Development Studies(8) is well on its way in cataloguing ongoing research projects in European countries that do not so far provide their own registers(9); and A. F. I. R. D. (10), the French association started in conjunction with the European Association, is preparing the publication, before the end of 1976, of a roster of research in progress in France.

Further tasks in the field of documentation

Improving documentation of research in progress is merely one among the tasks of the working group "Documentation and Information", albeit a very important one.

The group proposes in addition to promote information exchanges especially regarding available publications (viz. the exchange of publications lists), information on publications with selective circulation and grey literature (conference documents, mimeographed materials, official pronouncements by public bodies, teaching aids, etc.), the compilation of a catalogue of all relevant European institutions, calendars of relevant meetings and events, a survey of training facilities for documentation officers from developing countries and the interchange of documentation experts. But the working group decided against inclusion in its plan of operations of a register of all development aid programmes and projects, although it recognized the importance of such an undertaking, since the majority of organizations that carry out such aid programmes and projects in developing countries were not members of EADI, information on such projects was only fractionally available and since a good deal of such information was treated as confidential(11).

B.   Collaboration in training

At both the Ghent and Linz Conferences the tasks of EADI in the field of training were discussed and a number of proposals were put forward.   Both conferences emphasized that the promotion of collaboration in the training in development theory and practice of experts from developing countries and from European nations constitutes an essential part of EADI's mandate(12), (13), (14).

The agenda of the working group on "Training"(15), which was formed in December 1975, includes improvements in mutual information concerning ongoing and projected training programmes and courses, exchanges of experience and of views pertaining to specific training problems, and the elaboration of proposals for inner-European and inter-regional collaboration and the implementation of such proposals.

The first job undertaken by the new group, a survey of training activities of EADI member institutes, was recently published(16). In view of the fact, however, that this preliminary survey does not provide potential trainees and scholarship-granting institutions in both European and Third World countries with the full scale and necessary detail of training opportunities available, the Executive Committee of EADI decided in July 1976 to investigate the possibility of drawing up a European register of training programmes and to approach suitable institutions willing to participate in this project. An important step in the same direction was taken by the French Association which published a catalogue giving full details of such programmes available in France(17).

Besides specific tasks aiming at improving mutual information and expanding collaboration among the training institutes, which will be taken up one after the other by the working group, the problem of selecting optimally suited locations for particular programmes is becoming a central issue in its deliberations. On the one hand there are weighty arguments in favour of conducting a larger part of total training activities in developing countries and reasons for carrying out specific courses in particular developing regions, while on the other hand some programmes might more advantageously be held in Europe. A number of institutes are presently relocating some of their courses to points in certain developing countries. Coming to grips with this problem, which could also contribute to the strengthening of institutions in the developing countries, will be one of the main points of the discussions touching on the nature of inter-regional collaboration with the sister associations in Africa, Asia and Latin America.

C.   Collaboration in development research

The European Association is faced with two basic problems of delimitation in respect of its research activities, both of them connected with how one sees the objectives of development research.

Inasmuch as research aims at making a contribution to a better understanding of the processes of development, the only feasible strategy is a multidisciplinary approach. Although members of

EADI are mostly social science oriented, a course of action is indicated that transcends the social sciences; natural science and technology-oriented research must be mobilized to the extent that it is willing to collaborate in such multidisciplinary effort. For the purpose of the practical work of EADI in the domain of development research, it follows from this basic stance that the composition of groups working on specific problem areas should include all those disciplines which the subject-matter under consideration and its relation to the overall development process indicate(18). The second basic problem concerns the definition of the concept of "development" and its geographical delimitations. In other words, should EADI concentrate on research pertaining to problems in developing countries only, or should the European Association assume the rôle of an institution concerned with the development problems of the world as a whole, regardless of whether they arise in the industrialized world, in developing countries or in the relationships between States or groups of States, and regardless of whether they are caused endogenously or exogenously.

These questions were answered on purely pragmatic reasoning. The fact being established nowadays that problems which affect developing countries are only partly caused by internal factors, it was decided that EADI could not confine itself to problems in developing countries(19). On the other hand EADI does not aspire to co-ordinate research on all conceivable problems affecting development in industrialized countries. Consequently, at the meeting held in Bergen on the invitation of the Chr. Michelsen Institute, in March 1976, the Executive Committee decided that for the time being, equal attention should be devoted to the relations between industrialized nations and developing countries, and to problems in the developing countries(20).

Modes of collaboration in research

A progressive conversion of the prevalent and long-established concurrence of development research into a common effort must be cautiously tackled and brought into operation step by step. After a preliminary survey of requirements it became obvious that a number of different mechanisms for collaboration in research must be evolved to meet distinctive types of needs. Such mechanisms may have to be changed in the light of accumulated experience. Until such further experience becomes available, the following types of working groups, reflecting diverse requirements, were instituted.

1. Preparatory groups

Where there are members who voice their interest in intensified collaboration in a certain problem area, or if the Executive Committee decides to launch an attempt at such intensification, one member, or a small group of members, will be requested to undertake the necessary inquiries and soundings.

What matters at this stage is that potential participants for the group are found, that suggestions for first steps are elaborated and circulated and that after contacts with interested researchers, the problem area to be covered is clearly circumscribed and a programme of work adopted. If sufficient interest has been established, a proposal for setting up a permanent group and a draft working programme is submitted to the Executive Committee for comments and/or approval.

Depending on the kind of co-operation envisaged problem-oriented working groups or co-operative research groups will be instituted.

2. EADI working groups

Co-ordination of information is still largely lacking in development research. Researchers working in a particular field are therefore genuinely in need of an assured, regular and more rapid flow of information on the work done in their fields within other institutes; they want to know what hypotheses are considered, what data are available, which methods are applied, what problems and difficulties are encountered and which interim results were obtained. To serve this need problem-oriented EADI working groups are being created, each concentrating on a specific problem area, who would spread information about its field of work on a continuous basis by such means as circular letters or an information bulletin to all its members and to other interested persons. Supplementing this flow of written information, they could arrange working meetings, seminars and conferences thus affording opportunities for discussions, the establishment of contacts, and exchanges which might eventually lead on to co-operative research efforts(21).

As these problem-oriented working groups are primarily intended to speed up and assure the flow of information, they should be open to all interested members of the association.

3. EADI co-operative research groups

Besides improving problem-oriented information exchange, the European Association aims at stimulating and/or facilitating collaborative research programmes and projects. The more so as the development problems to be tackled far exceed available research capacities, because many investigations necessitate empirical field work in more than one country, and last not least, because co-operative exertions can effect savings in resources that are, in any case, rather limited.

In a first phase the co-operative research groups instituted with these ends in view will try to find a common approach in dealing with their subject-matter; they would plot their common problem, co-ordinate proposed research methods, lay down a working programme and a time schedule, agree on a division of labour and try to secure the required finance. Later phases include the actual carrying out of the detailed research, the necessary harmonization at all stages, and finally the publication of the results of their co-ordinated labours(22). In view of these objectives of co-operative research groups, which necessitate agreement on many lines, it will necessarily be up to the discretion of the group to decide, who should be invited to participate in its work. In order to make the co-operative research groups useful to all members, the EADI-Bulletin will regularly report on the state of their work.

Initial priority areas for research co-operation

When deciding on the problem areas that should be given priority by EADI, the following points must be considered: have sister associations in Africa, Asia and Latin America or their member institutes indicated their interest? What work is presently being undertaken by European institutes? Have members voiced readiness to launch or interest to participate in a group on a specific issue? And, last but not least, which problem areas of importance for the development of the Third World and the world as a whole that have been largely neglected would justify or necessitate scientific investigation?

Following a survey conducted by Professor Dudley Seers, President of the Association, it was decided that EADI continue some of the efforts initiated at Ghent and Linz and that the feasibility of a number of new groups be investigated. The full list of problem areas either in progress or under investigation presently includes the following:

- Migration and development;
- Adjustment policies;
- Appropriate technologies;
- Income distribution;
- Transnational corporations;
- Women and development;
- New commodity policies;
- Economic integration and development;
- Rural development;
- Consumption styles;
- Inflation and monetary problems of developing countries;
- Public administration;
- Manpower and education;
- Aid quality and quantity;
- Regional disparities and regional planning;
- National and cultural identity;
- Europe, the Mediterranean region and the Middle East;
- Arms and the military in a development context;
- Tourism and development.

Since these decisions have been taken only recently, it is too early to know which of these initiatives will bear fruit and in what form(23).

III. PROSPECTS AND OUTLOOK

The main thrust of EADI's efforts during the first months of its existence have been devoted to the promotion of inner European co-operation. This part of its work will continue to absorb a considerable proportion of EADI's energies in the future.

A large part of EADI's efforts in the immediate future will concentrate on inter-regional and international co-operation. Two inter-regional conferences in August and September 1976(24), (25), will provide a good chance to analyse the process of regionalization in the social sciences in general and in development research and training in particular. The interchange on experiences and positions held between the representatives from the different regions, who will be responsible for future co-operative efforts should provide excellent opportunities to work out and agree on priorities and mechanics for inter-regional and international co-operation. The challenge, with which participants will be faced, consists in finding solutions, which will allow full development of the positive aspects of regionalization, i.e. the formation and wide acceptance of concepts, models and paradigms which would take full account of the distinctive situation in the respective regions, without at the same time sacrificing the advantages inherent in inter-regional and international co-operation.

Another aspect of future activities of EADI will consist in establishing regular contacts with inter-governmental organizations concerned with research as well as with research departments and research institutes of the United Nations and its Specialized Agencies which work in the development field.

In the field of documentation and information exchange - as in most other areas of EADI's concern - it is evident that EADI cannot go it alone. A first step towards inter-regional co-operation has been made with the setting up of an international information network on ongoing development research(26). Another step towards solving some of the problems in this field might consist in close co-operation with DEVSIS(27).

In summary, it can be said that the evolution of EADI up to now seems to indicate that a rather important potential for furthering development research and for serving the poor majority of the world has come into existence. Whether this potential can be fully developed and put to good use is a question which can only be answered in future years.

(1) EADI, the abbreviated version of the English designation of the "European Association of Development Research and Training Institutes" will serve to designate the association in other languages too.

(2) Europäische Vereinigung von Entwicklungs-forschungs- und Ausbildungsinstituten (EADI), Kärntner Strasse 25/6, A-1010 Vienna, Austria. Tel. (222) 52 16 81.

(3) Members of the Executive Committee:

President

DUDLEY SEERS
Institute of Development Studies at the University of Sussex, Brighton

Executive Secretary

ARNE HASELBACH
Vienna Institute for Development, Vienna

Representatives of Regional Associations

ABDALLA S. BUJRA
Council for the Development of Economic and Social Research in Africa (CODESRIA), Dakar

FRANCISCO DELICH
Consejo Latinoamericano de Ciencias Sociales (CLACSO), Buenos Aires

AGUSTIN KINTANAR
Association of Development Research and Training Institutes of Asia and the Pacific (ADIPA), Bangkok

Members

MICHAEL BOHNET
IFO-Institute for Economic Research, Munich

SERGIO BORTOLANI
Centre for Financial Assistance to African Countries (FINAFRICA), Milano

JACQUES DE BANDT
Institut de Recherche en Economie de la Production, Paris

JUST FAALAND
The Chr. Michelsen Institute, Bergen

BRUNO KNALL
South Asia Institute, Heidelberg

ARTHUR S. LIVINGSTONE
Department of Administrative Studies for Overseas Visiting Fellows, Manchester

PETER MANDI
Institute for World Economics of the Hungarian Academy of Sciences, Budapest

JEAN MASINI
Institut d'Etude du Développement Economique et Social, Paris

ZORAN POPOV
Institut Ekonomikih Nauka, Beograd

C.A.O. VAN NIEUWENHUIJZE
Institute of Social Studies, The Hague

PER MAGNUS WIJKMAN
Institute for International Economic Studies, Stockholm

BOGODAR T. WINID
Institute of African Studies, Warszawa

ROBERT WOOD
Overseas Development Institute, London

(4) "The New International Order and Development Research and Training in Europe", Report on the 1975 General Conference of EADI, Linz, Austria, 11-13 September 1975, Ed. by Arne Haselbach, Executive Secretariat, EADI, Vienna, 1976, 133 p.

(5) See: "EADI Constitution" (adopted by the Constituent General Assembly, 12 September 1975, Linz, Austria), Ed. EADI, Vienna, 1975.

(6) "Second National Development Research Conference", 20-22 September 1973 at the University of East Anglia, organized by the Institute of Development Studies, Sussex, in co-operation with the Overseas Development Group of the University of East Anglia.

(7) The other conferences organized by the Vienna Institute for Development in its series of conferences at Linz were: "Deutschsprachige Entwicklungsforschung" (Development Research in the German Language Medium), 8-10 September 1975;

"SID-Council Meeting", 14 September 1975;

"World Structures and Development - Strategies for Change" (SID European Regional Conference 1975), 15-17 September 1975.

(8) This team is led by Dr. Mathew Tharakan, Centre d'Etudes du Développement, UFSIA-University, Antwerp, 13 Prinsstraat, B-2000 Antwerp, Belgium.

(9) The results of an extensive Norwegian survey undertaken at the behest of NORAD were

published in 1975, by the Institute for Studies in Research and Higher Education, Oslo, under the title, "Research relevant to Developing Countries - A Catalogue of Research Projects concerning Developing Countries at Norwegian Universities and Research Institutes".

(10) Association Française des Instituts de Recherche sur le Développement (AFIRD), 58 bd. Arago, F-75013 Paris, France.

(11) For more detailed information on EADI activities in the field of documentation, see inter alia:

"Report of the 1975 meeting of the working group Information and Documentation of the European Association of Development Research and Training Institutes, organized by the German Foundation for International Development", Bonn, DSE, 11-12 November 1975; and

"EADI-Bulletin" 1/1976, mimeo Vienna 1976, pp. 5-7 and 11-15.

(12) "Proposed Activities for the European Association", by C.A.O. van Nieuwenhuijze (as of March 1974), in: "Towards a European Association of Development Research and Training", EADI, Ghent, 1975, pp. 86-94.

(13) "Problèmes d'enseignement", Note de Jean Masini (IEDES), EADI General Conference 1975, Linz, Austria, Conference Document Nr. 7 - f.

(14) "Collaboration on Training" by Sergio Bortolani (FINAFRICA), EADI General Conference 1975, Linz, Austria, Conf. Doc. Nr. 1 - e.

(15) The working group is under the direction of Sergio Bortolani (FINAFRICA, Milano), Arthur S. Livingstone (Manchester University) and Jean Masini (IEDES, Paris).

(16) This preliminary summary of training activities of the member institutes of EADI is contained in the "EADI-Bulletin" 2/1976, pp. VII-XII, Vienna, 1976.

(17) "Répertoire des Enseignements sur le Développement dans les Universités et Instituts Français en 1975-1976" in: "Bulletin de Liaison", Nr. 1, January 1976, Association Française des Instituts de Recherche sur le Développement, Paris.

(18) "Programme of Activities as approved at the Ghent Conference", in: "Towards a European Association of Development Research and Training Institutes", op. cit., p. 98.

(19) A reference to Third World Development which was contained in the provisional title of the European Association, was turned down at Ghent. See: "Towards a European Association of Development Research and Training Institutes", op. cit., p. 35.

(20) See "Third Meeting of the Executive Committee", in "EADI-Bulletin" 2/1976, pp. II-IV.

(21) The Working Group "Migration and Development" is the most advanced example of a problem-oriented working group. It is directed by a geographically well balanced core group consisting of four persons, which has already produced three issues of its own information bulletin which is distributed to well over one hundred interested scientists and research institutes in Europe and the Mediterranean area; in addition, the group conducts a series of meetings and seminars.

(22) The group "Adjustment Policies" is an example of a functioning co-operative research group. It completed its first phase with a publication on "Adjustment for Trade - Studies on Industrial Adjustment Problems and Policies", OECD Development Centre, Paris, 1975, and is presently drafting the working programme for its second phase.

(23) Those interested in participating in any of these groups or in starting additional groups are requested to notify the Executive Secretariat, EADI, Kärnter Strasse 25/6, A-1010 Vienna, Austria; Tel. (0222) 52 16 81.

(24) "Meeting on Inter-regional Co-operation in the Social Sciences", Unesco, Paris, 23-27 August 1976.

(25) "First Inter-regional Meeting on Development Research, Communication and Education", at the Institute of Development Studies, University of Sussex, England, 12-16 September 1976.

(26) The "International Information Network on Development Research" was created recently by the four regional associations ADIPA, CLACSO, CODESRIA and EADI with the assistance of the OECD Development Centre.

(27) For background information concerning the "Development Sciences Information System - DEVSIS" see "EADI-Bulletin" 1/1976, pp. 34-38.

CHAPTER 8

The Developing Countries and Inter-Regional Co-operation in the Social Sciences

Samy Friedman
Secretary-General,
International Social Science Council

The ISSC has been invited by Unesco to express its views on inter-regional scientific co-operation in the light both of the contributions prepared for the August meeting on the subject of regional co-operation and of its own experience in the development of co-operation in the social sciences between the various regions of the world. Such an approach seems fully justified, for inter-regional co-operation is in no sense an independent intellectual category that can be referred to in isolation from national and regional factors. It is, or can only be, the extension of these.

It represents, in other words, the third storey of an edifice, the first two storeys of which are formed by national and regional infrastructures, in so far as these have come to terms with the constraints inherent in the present state of the social sciences and in the resources that are harnessed to ensure their development.

We therefore consider it vital, with the authors of the contributions submitted, to begin by analysing these constraints and their impact on the present state of the social sciences, from the standpoint, more especially, of the developing countries. We shall then go on to make an analysis of the criticisms levelled at the main approaches to the social sciences as these are asserted more particularly in the developed countries, and of the nature of the background to the social sciences in the developing countries. We shall then attempt to draw conclusions from this twofold analysis with regard to the objectives to be pursued in order to achieve inter-regional scientific co-operation, and with regard to its instruments and the means of implementation.

I. CRITICISM OF THE PRESENT STATE OF THE SOCIAL SCIENCES

In approaching the problem of inter-regional co-operation through study of the contributions presented, one is struck by the fairly general expression of dissatisfaction in regard to the nature and development of the main social science disciplines.

Strong criticism is made of these sciences from at least four points of view, which we shall deal with in turn.

(1) The first criticism concerns the "dominant paradigms". Ramashray Roy stresses the limits of these paradigms and the fact that they are ill-suited to conditions prevailing in the developing countries. Ahmad Khalifa, for his part, criticizes the predominance of Parsonian variables and Mertonian "rôle theory" in studies of social change. "In the best American spirit" he writes, "rôle differentiation and increased individualism become indices of modernity" and cease to be the reflection of the capitalist society that gave rise to these concepts. Dharam Ghai characterizes this situation as "fragmented, compartmentalized, and oriented towards routine micro-studies" (quoted by F. Alger and Gene M. Lyons in Int. Soc. Sc. Journal XXVI, No. 1, 1974, p. 142).

Similarly, Théodore Papadopoullos (and he is not alone in this) criticizes the functionalist theory of the human sciences, protesting against its "axiological claim" and the unwarranted projection of the "notion of justification into the virtual assertion of the goodness of cultural values" ("Anthropological Criteria for a Nation of Progress", Diogenes (91) 1975, pp. 54-55). Again, Floyd Merrell reproaches the new structuralist "rage" for being in reality the "stepchild of the classical model / i.e. static / of the universe", ("Structuralism and Beyond", Diogenes (92) 1975, p. 84). And Kaarle Nordenstreng, criticizing the current "communications" theory, considers that "the new approach in communication research as well as boosting interest in communication policies can be seen to reflect the same basic tendency of having the mechanism of the prevailing social order brought up to date, and thus supporting the basic tendencies of the status quo" ("Recent Developments in European Communications Theory", idem, p. 115).

In a still more general vein, Johan Galtung

in his book Theory and Methods of Social Research (London, Allen and Unwin, 1970) thinks that at the present stage of their development, the behavioural sciences are in many respects open to criticism. He says that "too much precision / is / misplaced on trivial matters", and that there is "too little respect for crucial facts as against grand theories, too much respect for insights that are common-place, too much indication and too little proof, too little genuine cumulation of generalizations, far too much jargon", etc. More especially he considers that the main obstacle to the progress of the social sciences lies in the dogma of the supposed value-neutrality of the social sciences in general, and of sociology in particular, vis-à-vis human values, ideologies and Utopias.

It can be shown that Galtung is not alone in these views merely by quoting an almost random selection of evidence taken from views expressed by French, German and American research workers. We find Jacqueline Feldman, for example, who came to sociology from physics, criticizing the "clumsy mimetism of science" and the "misuse of mathematics" by sociologists ("Sociologie, mathématique et science", Soc. Sc. Inform., 11 (3/4) June-August 1972 pp. 37-67), Rolf Klima stating that in the Federal Republic of Germany, "theoretical pluralism has led to anomia in the sociological world of this country" ("Theoretical pluralism, methodological dissension and the rôle of the sociologist: The West German Case", idem, pp. 69-108) and Alfons Silbermann echoing this view: "the real, important problems of our society are swept under the carpet, as armchair discussions continue .... To offset this we have, on the one hand, any amount of what Wright Mills and Hazel Henderson call "quantification freaks", on the other, a return to the good old German tradition of social philosophizing, coupled with an antiquated stock of ideas dressed in terms fresh from America" ("How sick is sociology in the Federal Republic of Germany?" Int. Soc. Sc. Journal, XXVII No.4), 1975, pp. 787-789). And, in a seminar held in Bellagio, Lazarsfeld observed that the "prevalence of quantitative methodology" in the United States was, in fact a recent phenomenon and what was needed was "a movement from quantitative to qualitative methodologies through the deepening of contemporary description with historical connexions, the linking of micro-macro relationships and the use of intuition and introspection to relate quantitative techniques to qualitative methodologies". (Alger and Lyons, op. cit. p. 143.)

(2) Second criticism: the ideological slant. Mpekesa Bongoy explains with feeling that "social science research institutes and organizations established in Africa were integrated with those in the colonizing countries and were used either as sources of basic data for processing in the mother country or as training grounds for young foreign research workers". He adds that "The activities of these research institutions and organizations were not primarily aimed at seeking ways and means of improving the social condition of the inhabitants of the colonized countries. In fact the contrary was often the case and some of the social research carried out was designed to obtain better knowledge of the psychological, temperamental, economic and other weaknesses of the inhabitants in order to accentuate these weaknesses and so perpetuate the stranglehold and domination of the colonial power. There are countless examples of this type of study ...".

(3) Third criticism: cultural and institutional dependence. We know, merely to take the example of French-speaking black Africa, that Africanist research has been focused more especially on traditional themes from ethnology, folklore, musicology or linguistics. It is only recently that studies have been carried out in economics, political science or sociology. A similar situation prevailed for many years in English-speaking Africa and in Asia. This dependence of the social sciences in the developing countries, linked, moreover, with a more general dependence - that of the Third World vis-à-vis the industrialized countries - and with the asymmetry of international relations, was studied at length during a seminar held in Bellagio from 19 to 21 July 1973, a summary of which is given by Chadwick F. Alger and Gene M. Lyons in the International Social Science Journal (XXVI No. 1, 1974).

We quote, in particular, these significant lines: "Dependency relations in the social sciences are an outgrowth of colonial empires whose institutions persist even after the political independence of countries of Africa and Asia. More recently they have grown up as an adjunct to the efforts of great powers to influence the economic, political and social development of nations within their spheres of influence. Dependency is also a consequence of the continued gap between developed and developing countries and the pressures on the small number of social scientists in developing countries to take on administrative and political responsibilities which reduce the time and resources they can devote to advanced research and teaching". (Chadwick F. Alger and Gene M. Lyons - "Social Science as a transnational system", Int. Soc. Sc. Journal, XXVI No. 1, 1974, p. 138.)

It was also pointed out at the same meeting, with justification, that "the dependency relation was also described in terms of an unequal exchange between social scientists in developed and less-developed countries, remarkably similar to unequal exchange in trade and commerce. Developing countries become resource bases to exploit sources of information processed abroad after being gathered and refined into elaborate hypotheses far from the original site ... all one has here is one-way dependence, the importation of theories, methods and philosophies of science and export of hardly anything, or occasionally of primary products, i.e. raw data, as opposed to the "high technology" exports of theories and methods" (Ibid., p. 138).

This "unequal exchange" derives first of all from the fact that social scientists in the developed countries carry out numerous studies in the developing countries, but the reverse rarely occurs. The situation was summed up in a terse phrase by Rodolfo Stavenhagen: "they study us, but we don't study them". Furthermore, the fact that many specialists in the developing countries have carried out their higher studies in the developed countries often has the effect of making them identify themselves more closely with the social science of these countries, seek the approval of their colleagues in the developed countries rather than that of their fellow-countrymen and in this way they tend to constitute an élite that has access to resources and facilities which are not available to their colleagues working in their country of origin.

Syad Hussein Alatas has recently proposed a reinterpretation of the concept of dependence, giving it greater force and terming it the "captive mind": see his articles "The captive mind in development studies", Int. Soc. Sc. Journal, XXIV No. 1, 1972, pp. 9-25, and "The captive mind and creative development", Int. Soc. Sc. Journal, XXVI No. 4, 1974, pp. 691-700.

He has dealt more particularly with what he calls "the inadequacies of current models and analyses uncritically derived from Western scholars and social science" (1972, p. 20) in the study of developing areas and he says that "what we need are alternative models, methodologies and concepts to modify, supplement, or substitute those already available". Two years later, he states that the problem is not to avoid Western science but, on the contrary, to assimilate it in a selective and constructive manner. The sciences have been developed in contemporary Western civilization: their generally valid, universal aspects have simply to be separated from their particular association with Western society. This author thus criticizes social science methodologies and models as they have taken shape in the Western world; this leads us to our next point.

(4) Domination of Western-developed theories and methodologies. In his working paper, Ramashray Roy lays considerable stress on the dominance of theories and methodologies derived from the experiences of the industrialized countries which, he states, still remain the major characteristic of the transnational social science system and which, since they are derived from the cultural tradition and historical experiences of the West, are ill-suited to the study of conditions prevailing in the less-developed countries. He also refers to the proceedings of the Bellagio seminar which we have already mentioned. He goes on to make two kinds of criticism of these dominant theories and methodologies:

(a) since they are derived from the cultural tradition and historical experiences of the industrialized societies, they are not helpful in making appraisal of, and suggesting remedies for, continuing anomalies in the developing countries;

(b) the thrust of empiricism in social science research with its emphasis on the construction of a grand theory restricts the choices available to research strategy as well as the explanatory framework for understanding social reality, since a general theory fails to take into account the variability of human situations and experience.

No-one would think of denying that the social sciences (which, even though not actually born in the West - their precursors can be found in Arab culture with Ibn Khaldun, or Chinese culture, with Sun Tsu - have at least been established as independent sciences there) have, by the very force of circumstances, developed methods and theories essentially based on the data and experience of the industrialized countries, or that they have been (and are still) governed by ideologies constructed on the basis of the situations, conflicts, praxis and thinking of these countries. Extremely detailed and specific criticisms of such presuppositions have been made by many eminent "Western" authors: one of the most interesting, for example, comes from Gunnar Myrdal, "Cleansing the approach from biases in the study of underdeveloped countries", Soc. Sc. Inform., 8 (3) June 1969, 9-26 (this is the introductory chapter to his book The Challenge of World Poverty). However, what Lévi-Strauss says of anthropology is perhaps true of other social sciences: "There would never have been any anthropology ... if a vast portion of humanity had not been dominated by another; if for decades and even centuries, men had not ravaged the natural resources of others and exterminated them, intentionally or not ..." ("Anthropology", Diogenes, (90) 1975, p. 23). But he goes on: "It would be unwarranted and incorrect to say that anthropology served the interests of colonialism; it did, however, take advantage of the situation and develop in its shadow. On an epistemological level, the effort to study man objectively undeniably reflects a situation in which one part of humanity is controlled by another. It would be absurd to hold this against anthropology today, just as it would be to neglect the discoveries in physics or biology that were made on the basis of wartime technology. In a similar vein, astronomers might be accused of lending support to the capitalist system because their telescopes are made by workers who do not control their productive labour" (pp. 23-24).

It is, perhaps, dangerous to yield to the

temptation to "throw the baby out with the bath-water" and to reject all "Western" social science theories and methods on the grounds that they have been developed in the West. In his inaugural address at the Asian Conference on Teaching and Research in Social Sciences (Simla, May 1973), Sukhmoy Chakravarty, as Yogesh Atal reports (p. 14 of the Proceedings) expressed his disagreement with "the argument advanced by scholars who over-emphasize the fact of historical specificity". He stated: "It is often maintained that Asian societies are different from European societies and hence, training and research in social sciences in Asian countries will have to be different in character. On one level, the argument means nothing more than a recognition of historically specific factors in dealing with a particular society - social sciences cannot be discussed in isolation from history. There is nothing to dispute about this interpretation. However, there is a much more far-reaching interpretation which goes beyond the recognition of historically relevent circumstances pertaining to a society and would amount to a rejection of any element of universality in a social science. In my opinion, such interpretations cannot be sustained on methodological grounds" (p. 33).

We shall come back to the question of "indigenization" which is very closely bound up with this discussion of methods and theories. But it is worth while quoting once again from Atal's introduction to Social Science in Asia (p. 21): "research carried out in these /Asian / societies - either by local scholars or by foreign scholars - follows the models and the methodology developed in the West. When data are acquired through procedures which may be questionable, and when they are analysed in terms of the imported conceptual scheme evolved without any regard to the empirical reality, distortions are bound to occur. The philosophy of cultural relativism notwithstanding, outside researchers unconsciously inject their biases in the research reports". It may also be observed that local researchers themselves may be influenced, consciously or otherwise, by theories that do not fully fit the facts and which they have learned during their studies abroad or from imported textbooks. And Atal goes on to draw attention to the fact that social scientists in the Asian region sometimes "indulge in the exercise of one-sided accentuation". At times their assertions become synchronized with political decisions "to keep foreigners out".

In such circumstances indigenization begins to appear chauvinistic. He quotes the resolutions adopted at Simla which are, in fact, far from adopting this kind of "narrow nationalism".

II.   THE ENVIRONMENT OF THE SOCIAL SCIENCES IN THE DEVELOPING COUNTRIES

The environment in the developing countries itself impedes the development of the social sciences in many ways. Chief among the impediments are:

(1)   Anti-scientific traditions

As Ramashray Roy observes in his working paper, basing himself at the same time on Durkheim, two conditions must be fulfilled if a scientific sociology is to come into existence: (1) the disintegration of traditionalism, and (2) faith in the power of reason, of science, to examine social realities and, ultimately, to change them. These two conditions, Roy adds, have been lacking in Asia where social forms were "taken for granted" although subject to occasional political turbulences. Societies that are "taken for granted" contribute nothing to the social sciences. In a number of developing countries, opposition to the creation of a "scientific community" - and this does not only apply to the social sciences - still comes from what may be termed "anti-scientific" traditions (which are, incidentally, re-emerging in the West with the anti-science movement, particularly among young people). The situation in Islam is described in the work of G. Luftiya, Baytin (The Hague, Mouton, 1966); for India, see what A. Rahman has written on "commitment to science and the scientific attitude" which deals more particularly with the natural sciences but can also be applied to the social sciences (in his article "Scientists in India", Int. Soc. Sc. Journal, XXII No. 1, 1970, cf. pp. 74-77).

(2)   Lack of relevance in training

The teaching of the social sciences is often ill-suited to national conditions: see, for example, Jean Coussy's case study "Adjusting economics curricula to African needs", Int. Soc. Sc. Journal, XXI No. 3, 1969, pp. 393-405. At the same time, there exists in many, if not all, developing countries what Roy describes as a "duality" between teaching which proceeds on traditional lines, and research, based on theories and methodologies developed in recent years. This duality is all the more accentuated since universities, in general, "impart a routine science which requires no original research or creative thinking". As there is an acute shortage of textbooks and basic study material in the language or languages of the home country, young Ph. D's who, during their stay abroad, have concentrated in their academic work on study of their country of origin, find themselves, on returning home, completely taken up with the task of writing books for students, to the neglect of research work which would require, moreover, much more time and effort than they can devote to it (cf. the working paper by A. M. Khalifa whose views tie up with those of Ayad Al-Qazzaz, "Impressions of Sociology in Iraq", Int. Soc. Sc. Journal, XXVII No. 4, 1975, pp. 784-785).

(3)   The pressure of national development

The "pressure of national development" may itself
act as a constraint, as regards both progress in
the social sciences in national terms and increased
co-operation at the inter-regional level: on this
point see Roy's working paper, "The pressure of
national development".

Rigid disciplinary compartmentalization in
universities, as well as their marked slant towards
teaching to the detriment of R&D, have in many
instances brought about the creation, in the developing countries, of research institutes outside the
university structures.   Such institutional development has led, at least in some countries (Egypt
for example), to the setting up of pluri-disciplinary
teams able to carry out valid research (cf. Khalifa).
However, even these institutes have often had to
contend with difficult problems, particularly as
regards the tendency of many governments to
insist on research, the applications of which provide an immediate "return" and are "relevant" to
development requirements, regardless of the fact
that there is often a danger of ending up (as Al-
Qazzaz points out in connexion with Iraq, p.783)
with "library works" or "simple statistical des-
criptions of the phenomena in question", studies
which are meant "for use by the appropriate government agencies".   It may also happen that very
few of these research studies are actually used by
the "consumers" - the political decision-makers,
government administrations, etc.   Moreover such
research rarely serves as "teaching input"
(M.S. Adiseshiah, Presidential Address, Proceedings of the Asian Conference on Teaching and Research in Social Sciences, Simla, p.43).   "Applied"
research in response to "short-term demands"
will take too much precedence over "basic" research (cf. Oscar Cornblit, "Factors affecting
scientific productivity: the Latin American case",
Int. Soc. Sc. Journal, XXII No.2, 1970, pp.251-252).

(4)   Isolation and lack of critical mass

Although in the developed countries the social
science researcher is less and less an isolated
individual, the "research leaders" being backed
up by teams of collaborators - particularly advanced
students preparing their doctorate - the same does
not usually apply in the developing countries.
Comparison should be made for example between
the development of sociological research on a collaborative basis in the United States (see Narsi
Patel, "Collaboration in the professional growth
of American sociology", Soc. Sc. Inf., 12 (6)
Dec. 1973, pp.77-92), and the individual research
conditions in South East Asia (Peter D. Weldon,
"Teaching and research in sociology in South East
Asia", idem, 12 (5) Oct. 1973, pp.143-156:   more
especially p.152).

In the developing countries there is rarely a
sufficient "critical mass" for "modern" research,
i.e., for research that is interdisciplinary and has
adequate resources for investigation and interpretation, calculation and simulation, etc., and which
also perhaps, as Storer writes, (Norman W. Storer,
"The internationality of science and the nationality
of scientists", Int. Soc. Sc. Journal, XXII No. 1,
1970, p. 92) has "an audience of sufficient size and
competence to provide adequate feedback - professional recognition - to its members so that they
need not feel totally dependent upon feedback from
abroad" (Storer has the natural and physical sciences in mind, but this view applies equally to the
social sciences).   Among the reports prepared for
the meeting, Ramashray Roy's paper emphasizes
this notion of "critical mass" and his observations
on this subject are very much to the point.

(5)   Ideological conflict and domestic policy

It may also be the case that in certain countries
social crisis and the internal ideological and political conflicts to which it gives rise militate against
the greater institutionalization of the social sciences
and of sociology in particular, regarded as it frequently is as being "subversive" (see, in the case
of Latin America, Aldo E. Solari "Social crisis as
an obstacle to the institutionalization of sociology
in Latin America", Int. Soc. Sc. Journal, XXI
No. 3, 1969, pp.445-456:   cf. his conclusion that
"A discipline cannot be fully institutionalized when
there are a large number of factors tending to
divide its practitioners with regard to its meaning
and the line it should follow").

(6)   Inadequate resources

A point has been raised by André Béteille ("The
dangers of research methodology", Int. Soc. Sc.
Journal XXVIII No. 1, 1976, pp.195-197) who
observes that, at least in India, "the best results
were achieved in the past before the new methodology /i.e. that of American sociological research/
came into vogue;   the results that have followed
from its application have so far been very meagre
indeed".   He asks if "the technical apparatus of
research" has been used meaningfully or whether
there has not been "disproportion between the problems to be studied and the apparatus mobilized for
their study", if "the needs of the apparatus itself
do not tend to divert the attention of scholars from
the direct pursuit of relevant sociological problems"
and he fears that "niceties of methodology" tend
"to become an end in themselves, and hence a
source of distraction".   In addition, he argues,
"the new technology of research is costly.   It is
best suited to large research projects for which
abundant funds are available... Observers in backward countries must consider with some misgiving
the possibility that the preoccupation with the most
'advanced' technology of research might generate
its own pressures in favour of expensive projects".
This argument is no doubt open to question.

Because a technique is costly, that does not mean, in principle, that it is necessarily unreasonable to use it in a developing country. But there is however one point in this connexion that ought to be considered: there may be a case, in line with current support for the use in the developing countries of "intermediate technologies" better adapted to the solution of their pressing problems than certain advanced techniques, for looking into the possibility of using "intermediate technologies" in social research.

It is still a fact, however, that financial resources are, in general, woefully inadequate in the developing countries.

M. S. Adiseshiah in his Presidential address to the first Asian Conference on Teaching and Research in Social Sciences (Simla, May 1973: see Proceedings edited by Yogesh Atal, Social sciences in Asia, New Delhi, 1974, p.47) stressed this inadequacy of resources in regard to India, a country where, nevertheless, the social and human sciences are, relatively speaking, in a stronger position than in certain other developing countries: out of an annual R&D budget of 2,500 million Rs., only 25 million Rs., was being spent on the social sciences. Adiseshiah says that this "is a serious imbalance" and suggests that by the end of the Second Development Decade, 5-6 per cent of the 1 per cent GNP research target should be allocated to social science research.

It would not be difficult to give a host of similar examples.

III. THE OBJECTIVES OF INTER-REGIONAL CO-OPERATION IN THE SOCIAL SCIENCES

The developments outlined above seem to us to point to the directions towards which inter-regional co-operation in social sciences should move, on condition that at the national level a simultaneous effort is made to attempt to alleviate, if not to overcome, the difficulties and obstacles hampering the progress of the social sciences.

What has to be created first of all in the developing countries is a climate which is increasingly conducive to social science teaching and research. This will become established as anti-scientific traditions die away, as teaching shows greater regard for local needs, and as governments display a willingness both to ensure sufficient funds for R&D and to curb their impatient demands for the instantaneous achievement of immediately usable results. The social sciences offer no panaceas for the ills that beset the developing countries. To demand too much of them too rapidly is to risk curbing their impetus and preventing any real progress.

The developing countries must then realize that their present state of dependence vis-à-vis Western science is in no way permanent and irremediable, and that, on the contrary, the pursuit

of certain regional and inter-regional co-operation objectives may make it possible both to reinforce their own infrastructure and to ensure the advance of knowledge more closely linked with conditions existing in these countries.

Subject to that, it ought to be possible to achieve success in three different directions:

(1) Indigenization

Ramashray Roy's working paper seems to provide a good point of departure for discussion on this subject, particularly in the third section on "Trends towards indigenization". Roy's basic thesis is that indigenization "is a necessary step towards putting the social sciences in a larger frame of reference, provided by inter-regional co-operation". He goes on to say that "the movement of 'indigenization' and 'regionalization' ... creates environments within which dominant theories and methodologies can be more critically tested, evaluated and improved upon than ever before. It also provides opportunity for genuine international exchange based on a candid confrontation of diverse world views drawn from diverse historical and institutional experiences. Seen in this perspective, such a movement does not pose any target to universality of knowledge; what it, however, does is to transform the centre-periphery relationship that exists now into a poly-centric world of social sciences".

In the light of what has been stated in the first part of this document, the principle underlying this thesis can hardly be disputed. However, "indigenization" undeniably poses considerable problems. It implies the creation of an infrastructure which, in many cases, is still only in embryonic form - the infrastructure of teaching and of research (problem No. 1 in the list of "Main problems in the development of sociology" in the survey carried out by Weldon in South East Asia, op. cit., p.154, was the "lack of trained teaching personnel"). It is governed by critical reflection on the question of adjusting theories and methods to local conditions. It must avoid nationalism and, particularly, narrow chauvinism; the predominance of premature applications over basic research; the diverting of "highly qualified manpower" to ancillary extension work tasks or to positions in which they are well paid but hampered by "technocrats" ...

(2) Relevance

Of more fundamental importance, perhaps, is the need - which we have already met - to seek "relevance" in research, its liaison with development policy targets and its relation with the burning social issues of the society in which it is conducted. As A. M. Khalifa writes, "The promotion of the contending sociology /̄ and this is true not only of sociology / has brought in its trail a number of new sociological instruments for investigation. The penetration of the political and social militant spirit among sociologists has changed the trends of development and the contemporary sense of sociology".

However, at the end of his report, Khalifa seems to voice a doubt when he writes: "Our society is in a state of turmoil and a soul-searching process is well on: are we producing the type of data or using methodology that best fits our developmental needs?" Perhaps not always, but it is precisely here that an effort is both necessary and possible. Two lines of approach have to be adopted. The first is not to endeavour to transpose foreign models systematically where there are insufficient developed statistical infrastructures but, instead, to attempt to develop simpler methodologies in order to come to grips with social reality. Demographic or public opinion studies in the less advanced countries provide good examples of such a course of action. The second would consist, as we have already briefly indicated, in discarding the search for grand theories and concentrating on those of medium scope and on intermediate technologies. In line with Merton's approach, these include theories bringing into play a limited number of interdependent concepts and providing a basis for framing various hypotheses that are verified empirically in well-defined situations.

(3) Cross-national studies

It is a fact that cross-national and cross-cultural studies were due, at the outset and still largely remain due, to the initiative of social scientists in the developed countries. And, if one examines a document such as that of the National Academy of Sciences - The Behavioral and Social Sciences: Outlook and Needs (Washington, 1969), Chapter 16 of which deals with "World development of social sciences" (pp. 250-260) - one sees that its conclusions (which go back, it is true, six years) are confined to considerations which might be described as "ethical": associating local specialists in the work of American researchers operating in foreign countries, clearly indicating the origin of funds ... The difficulties of the "unequal yoking" of national and foreign research workers have been well presented by Prodipto Roy and Frederick C. Fliegel in "The conduct of collaborative research in developing nations: the insiders and the outsiders", Int. Soc. Sc. Journal, XXII No. 3, 1970, pp. 505-523 (see in particular pp. 512, 518-519).

It is worth while consulting Stein Rokkan's chapter, still a fundamental text, on "Cross-cultural, cross-societal and cross-national research" in Main Trends of Research in the Social and Human Sciences (Unesco, 1970, I, pp. 645-689), in which the author clearly spells out the essential theoretical problem which is that of knowing how far the "universalist assumptions" underlying the majority of cross-cultural studies carried out so far are a valid basis for comparisons "across societies differing so fundamentally in structure

and in ethos" (p. 667). He has also stated the principle whereby "Cross-national research requires an institutional framework, an organizational basis. Great plans and important pilot studies may be born of haphazard encounters between enthusiasts, but a cumulative tradition of cross-national research can develop only within a clear-cut organizational setting" (p. 678).

In his report for the meeting in August 1976, Roy has pointed out some of the obstacles to the development of valid cross-national studies in the developing countries: (1) the fact that research often bears on themes that reflect the concerns of the "academic centres" of the developed countries which participate in such studies and more or less decide on their content; (2) the preponderance in the developing countries of "micro-studies" - "A heavy reliance on such studies has precluded a macro-social perspective which is essential for understanding the enlarged networks of relationships that affect smaller units. It also precluded the emergence of a comparative method vital for understanding macro-social complexes"; (3) the barriers to inter-communication between researchers in developing countries (even in the case of adjacent countries) and, on the other hand, the existence of "non-communicating 'corridors'" which linked the intelligentsia of each colony to some distant intellectual centre of gravity in the Occident. Their 'underdeveloped' neighbours were of no interest" (quoted from Ralph Pieris).

But these obstacles are not insurmountable and Unesco might very well encourage a series of comparative, cross-national studies on social science teaching and research in different continents, bearing especially on: (1) the way in which the social sciences have been established, having regard to the prevailing ideologies and asymmetry in intellectual relations in connexion with these sciences; (2) any practical contribution that the social sciences have made to the solution of problems raised in the regions in question by economic and social development. It would be worth while, we believe, for such studies and research to be conducted by teams consisting not only of specialists from the region or country concerned, but also specialists from other continents where similar problems arise in quite a different light. Comparison of these situations is bound to be extremely stimulating for both sides.

Other research themes that might serve as a basis for inter-regional co-operation come readily to mind. We shall mention some of these and, first of all, in the context of the general subjects of concern related to the establishment of a new world economic order, we would refer to the importance of studies on the development of enterprise and the spirit of enterprise.

We might consider here comparative studies in several continents between rural and urban communities where the spirit of enterprise and innovation has developed and others, outwardly similar, where this spirit is still wanting. Such research involves analyses bearing on the formation of capital, the dissemination of technical knowledge, the level of instruction associated with industrial and commercial management skills, and the opposition or stimulation resulting from the socio-cultural and religious situation of the communities concerned.

The making of comparative studies on social stratification and social mobility should also be encouraged, in connexion more particularly with the emergence of new classes and of new élites and the conflict situations entailed by socio-political change. The integration of customary law and modern codified law is another subject of great interest, particularly in Africa and Asia, as a result of the rapid development of codified law in line with the conditions of modern life (commercial law, contract law, civil liability, personal rights, land tenure system, etc.). The problems of the acceptance of new law and the points of convergence of the two legal systems warrant detailed examination.

Studies on work and workers, particularly as regards training matters and the rôle of trade unions whose opposition to the colonial system are not sufficiently well-known. There is also the question of the productivity of labour in relation to the attitudes and motivations of workers in different sectors of activity which also appears important from the point of view of social change and the introduction of a new economic order.

Generation conflict and youth attitudes, study of which might show how the political attitudes of students differ from those of the governing classes and from the outlook of young people in the developed countries. Analysis would doubtless reveal interesting regional variations and probably a more widespread respect for authority than is normally supposed. Studies of this type would, furthermore, be relatively simple to carry out for they use only accessible methodologies (surveys by questionnaire), producing readily comparable results.

Lastly, in continents in which the extreme youth of the population and problems of the emancipation of women are distinguishing features, these two groups should not be overlooked. Comparative development of child psychology and the social and psychological effects of the different language policies are of prime concern, for very often in Africa and in Asia - and in Latin America as well - young people embark on the learning process in a language that they have seldom heard or used outside school: Swahili in Tanzania, Cicewa, followed by English in Malawi, French in the French-speaking countries, Amhari in Ethiopia, Swahili, Tsiluba and Kikongo in Zaire, etc. The rôle that devolves upon women in the developing countries seems of vital importance and appears to be suitable for study by comparative methods. Too often up to now this question has been approached in the context of educational, urban or political surveys. The time has perhaps come to view the rôle of women in a broader, independent context.

IV. THE INSTRUMENTS OF INTER-REGIONAL CO-OPERATION

The documents prepared for the meeting in August 1976 do not seem to us to constitute an adequate basis for a serious critical evaluation of experience in co-operation at the regional level. What is more, in most cases (apart from Latin America, for which there is no working paper, and Europe) the institutions are too recent for such an evaluation to be carried out at the present stage.

Reference may be made to the article - which, though no longer recent is still useful - by Marie-Anne de Franz, "Implanting the social sciences - a review of Unesco's endeavours", Int. Soc. Sc. Journal, XXI No. 3, 1969, pp. 406-420, to the anonymous article "Regionalization of social sciences in Latin America, Asia and Africa", idem, XXV No. 4, 1973, pp. 557-560, and to the mimeographed documents quoted by Roy in his report.

In the absence of critical evaluation, some general, empirical findings can, however, be put forward. In Europe, the "Vienna Centre" (the European Co-ordination Centre for Research and Documentation in Social Sciences) can be described as a success, but this success is basically due to the fact that the Centre is founded on co-operation between research institutions that already exist - in some instances they are of long standing - are staffed by competent specialists (often interdisciplinary) and have sufficient funds available. Difficulties of an ideological and methodological kind have been overcome through joint efforts and through the adoption of empirical research procedures that have generally been agreed on during the research work itself. In Latin America FLACSO has also been a success, but in the training field and not in research: it has helped in creating a body of competent teachers and researchers, trained according to a standardized methodology.

Regional social science institutions in Asia and, more especially in Africa, certainly cannot as yet claim an equally favourable record. Difficulties are greater in those countries and are mainly connected with pre-existing national infra-structures and the influence of various factors outlined in the reports of Roy and Bongoy; by and large these difficulties can probably be attributed to one major circumstance: the aftermath of a relatively more recent colonial situation. As regards the Arab countries, A. M. Khalifa's working paper indicates clearly the set of complex reasons which so far appear to have hampered regional co-operation efforts.

Experience at the inter-regional level

Up to now there has virtually been no real "inter-regional co-operation" in social sciences, apart from individual initiatives, the participation of a few non-European countries in some of the Vienna Centre's research projects and - if this can be called "inter-regional co-operation" - the two examples of co-operation by the Social Science Research Council of the United States with certain European countries (with the European Association for Experimental Social Psychology and the Committee on Political and Social Science in Italy) and various bilateral or multilateral projects financed by the Ford Foundation (cf. the report of the National Academy of Sciences already quoted, pp. 253, 257-258) or by the National Institute of Mental Health of the United States (idem, p. 252).

Many of the activities of international associations in the social science disciplines and of the International Social Science Council can, however, be considered under the head of "inter-regional" co-operation in its broad sense, that is to say as international co-operation. More specifically, we can include in this category the seminars organized by various associations (economists' associations more especially) for the training of advanced students and research workers from the Third World countries, and similar seminars held by the International Social Science Council.

These various activities should be continued by the main "protagonists" of scientific co-operation.

(1) Regional social science councils

Regional social science councils undoubtedly have an important rôle to play in regional co-operation on social science research and teaching. A. Akiwowo argues that in Africa it would be preferable not to set up national councils but to establish an African social science council (of the CLACSO type). Some co-operation between councils might be contemplated, but this would probably be fairly limited and of a rather "traditional" character (fellowships, exchanges of teachers or research workers, and possibly translations...).

(2) Professional associations

Their information and training work can be of considerable importance, particularly if they are organized on a regional basis, along the same lines as CODESRIA, for example. We also have in mind the work of national professional associations, still too rare in the developing countries, the setting up of which in each of the main social science

disciplines should be encouraged. In this connexion it may be mentioned that certain international associations, including the International Sociological Association, have had the idea of decentralizing their activities to a certain extent by encouraging the creation of national groups affiliated to them. These measures should be encouraged in so far as it is possible to ensure that the new national bodies would not too rapidly be dominated by the international organization, whose prestige and resources might be likely to slow down the movement towards the goal of indigenization. We should like to see a reversal of this process with the establishment of national groups being encouraged before resorting to the affiliation procedure, which remains a desirable long-term objective. The Association africaine de sciences politiques seems to be an example of a move in the right direction.

The ISSC itself might consider developing its activities in regard to the developing countries on an inter-regional basis within the framework of the Standing Committees and, more especially, under the World Development of Social Science project, in collaboration with the associations for the social science disciplines which are members of the Council.

Lastly it is to be hoped that Unesco might support inter-regional co-operation projects by aiding specific programmes carried out jointly by regional councils, the Vienna Centre and the ISSC.

(3) Activities bearing on particular aspects

The Vienna Centre (see the report by its President, Adam Schaff, for the August 1976 meeting) has put forward some interesting proposals: (1) exchange of information; (2) possibility of accepting trainees and/or sending qualified research workers to other regions; (3) possibility of research undertaken in conjunction with research institutes in other regions.

These proposals warrant careful consideration and we have already shown that the time is now ripe for a series of comparative, cross-national studies to be made on current teaching and research practice in the social sciences in the various continents. Such studies, involving extensive co-operation, would help, furthermore, to develop a real international scientific community, which is still confined too much to the more advanced countries.

It would obviously be the rôle of the August 1976 meeting to assign priorities with a view to establishing such co-operation and to define the central, innovatory rôle that devolves on Unesco in this field.

CHAPTER 9

Priorities for Social Science Research in Developing Countries[1]
by the Unesco Secretariat

I

1. The present working paper has been prepared by the Unesco Secretariat. It is therefore
understandable that, in discussing social science
research priorities in the developing countries, it
will deal primarily with Unesco's experience in
this field. It is not within the scope of this review,
nor was it possible in view of the manner in which
it was prepared, to deal with research priorities
established and followed up by other bodies, such
as sister organizations of the United Nations system, various international associations, regional
organizations and national research institutions.
These priorities will be considered in the paper
only to the extent that they have a bearing on
Unesco's activities, be it with regard to the setting
of objectives, the carrying out of research, and to
the diffusing and utilizing of the research results.
Generally speaking, research priorities of other
bodies will serve as a basis of comparison, a back-
drop against which Unesco's own activities can be
more clearly outlined.

2. The paper will concentrate on the research
into social problems in the developing countries
undertaken and carried out within the social science programme of Unesco falling under the former
Department of Social Sciences. It would be clearly
impossible within the confines of a short paper to
deal with other fields of Unesco's work (education,
science, culture, communication) where a research
contribution from the social sciences might also be
involved. Besides, social science research in
these domains, if it exists, is rather of ancillary
nature.

3. The basic source for discerning Unesco's
social science research priorities in the developing countries are the decisions of the General
Conference. The paper will be concerned mainly
with those activities in the field of social research
in developing countries, which appear in successive
biennial programme and budget documents (C/5),
which are in fact nothing else than sets of priorities.

4. Unesco's biennial programmes are adopted
by each General Conference after a long process
of consultation with Member States, Associate
Member States and international non-governmental
organizations: projects are sifted and weighed
one against the other, and ultimately a decision
is taken on what new projects to introduce, on
those to be retained, on others to be modified and
yet others to be postponed or given up altogether.
Establishing priorities is to state preferences and,
like every choice connected with the allocation of
scarce resources, is a political act, unavoidably
bound up with value judgements. To reduce
possible differences of opinion and arrive at a
consensus, it is necessary to establish the criteria
on which the programme should be based, to apply
these criteria to specific proposals, and on this
basis to assign priorities to concrete projects.

5. There is no comprehensive statement or
resolution that sets out the criteria for setting
priorities for research programmes in the developing countries. However, a closer examination
of various Unesco documents yields the following
desiderata which underline the choice of programmes: (i) they should be urgently needed and
important for the economic, social and cultural
development of Member States; (ii) they should
be able to contribute to understanding and solving
important issues within the framework of national
development efforts; (iii) they should be in a field
in which progress can be significantly accelerated
by international and intergovernmental co-operation;
(iv) they should be realistic in terms of Unesco's
ability to carry them out within an appropriate
period of time; (v) they should play a significant
catalytic rôle or be capable of producing a multiplier effect.

II

6. There are three contexts in which Unesco's
social science programme in the developing

(1) This paper was prepared in September 1975.

countries operates and which have a definite bearing on research priorities: (i) the United Nations system; (ii) Member States; (iii) scientific community.

7. As regards the United Nations system there are three points of relevance: (i) the United Nations as a source of inspiration and guidelines (e.g. resolutions of the General Assembly, such as 3201 and 3202 (S-VI) on a New International Economic Order, and of the Economic and Social Council; recommendations of the United Nations World Conference, such as World Population Conference; World Food Conferences, etc.); (ii) collaboration with those units of the United Nations which deal with social problems (Department of Economic and Social Affairs, Regional Commissions and their specialized institutes - such as the United Nations Asian Institute for Economic Development and Planning, United Nations Research Institute for Social Development) as well as with other members of the United Nations family (FAO, ILO, Unicef, UNIDO, WHO); (iii) collaboration with agencies which fund certain Unesco activities (UNDP, UNFPA).

The main considerations are those of co-ordination and definition of competencies. First, no duplication of functions should exist since action is urgently needed and the resources available are inevitably limited. Second, Unesco should undertake these research activities that are truly distinctive to its own special character. The basic consideration here is that Unesco is the only agency within the United Nations system which has responsibility for fostering the growth of the social sciences in themselves and as a global enterprise. This involves the advancement of social science knowledge, communication and exchange of results of research within the framework of international intellectual co-operation.

The impact of the rest of the United Nations system on Unesco's research priorities is considerable and can be discerned in various programmes. The pattern is not uniform, though. The strongest and most direct influence is at play when research activities are financed by extra-budgetary sources (UNFPA, UNDP). This reliance on United Nations funding sources (UNFPA in the case of the population research, UNDP in the case of regional programmes of FLACSO and CLACSO in Latin America) can determine to a large extent the choice of research themes, the character and scope of research. Sometimes it implies not so much the definition of research priorities as co-operation concerning implementation at project level with other agencies and competent United Nations bodies (with ILO, as regards work on simulation models, with UNRISD and United Nations Statistical Commission, as regards social indicators).

8. As regards Member States, there is, first of all, a paramount necessity to ensure that the programmes adopted reflect the needs of Member States as accurately as possible. Significance and relevance as basic considerations for establishing research priorities at the national level can be judged in three contexts: (i) individual, (ii) disciplinary, (iii) social. Every piece of research is in the first place a matter of personal choice and commitment of individual social scientists; without their active involvement, the research cannot be carried out. These issues can also be judged according to the extent to which research results will prove significant for the promotion of a social science discipline (theory-building and/or methodological improvement). This point of view is usually represented by a professional association. Finally, significance and relevance can be defined in social terms, i.e. by indicating to what extent the research carried out will help understand and solve the issues of importance to a given society. Here it is a national body (often a government-sponsored research council) which is vested with the authority to decide the significance and relevance of a particular research programme for national needs. This is related - a pertinent consideration here - to the granting of financial support to research proposals. Of course, these three contexts are not always so clear-cut; they may mingle and overlap. Neither are they mutually exclusive; in most cases it is possible - at least, theoretically - to reconcile national priorities and the freedom of individual social scientists and the autonomy of research institutions. This normally implies building the necessary safeguards for academic freedom and institutional autonomy in the national policy for social science research itself. There is no doubt, however, that the prevalent attitude is to define significance and relevance in terms of its social importance. The overriding consideration is that large segments of the population have come to be concerned about a specific problem, and they have recognized that it cannot be resolved by individual choice or individual action.

Unesco is accountable to Member States and must see to it that their interests are being adequately understood or served. At the same time, the Organization is also accountable to the world community and must translate national concerns into regional and world-wide initiatives. It is necessary to strike a balance between national and international needs and priorities. In general, it is recognized by Member States that it is through international (regional) undertakings that national interests could very well be furthered and needs and priorities met. There is an awareness of a basic unity underlying socio-economic and cultural problems of each of the developing regions and perhaps of the Third World as a whole; it is acknowledged that social science research is by and large most economically developed on an inter-country basis; and that an international framework ensures a wider application of the results.

9. As regards Unesco's relations with the scientific community, it involves, on the one hand,

the closest contacts with international non-governmental organizations of specialists, on the other hand, co-operation with regional and national social science institutions, such as AASSREC in Asia, CLACSO and FLACSO in Latin America, CODESRIA in Africa.

Unesco's concern for the promotion of social science research in the developing countries is closely connected with the Organization's effort to develop the social sciences as a global enterprise. It is the need to give truly international scope to social science teaching and research which has called for building up the social sciences in those parts of the world where the social science infra-structure is at an early and fragmented stage of development.

Unesco's efforts in this regard have been accompanied by a recent but widely diffused development in social science circles of Latin America, Asia and Africa, called diversely "indigenization" or "regionalization" of social sciences, by contrast to the use of "imported" social science theories and models. The Organization is both influencing and being influenced by this course of events. It has taken the initiative in promoting this trend; at the same time, it learns from and adapts to the attitudes and aspirations of the developing countries, expressed by their social science institutions and scholars. The principle of "globalization" makes it necessary to arrange through Unesco and in other ways for social scientists from developing countries to take part as "full participants" at the cutting edge of contemporary research. The prin-ciple of "indigenization" implies in turn carrying out activities in developing areas, rather than simply equalizing the costs of participation in Europe and North America. The existence of indigenous resources and facilities as well as the conduct of research by local scholars on topics chosen on the spot and most relevant to the regions concerned, are considered the only way of assur-ing that research designs and findings would reflect the values and orientations and respond to the felt needs of the country (or groups of countries) in which the research takes place.

The process of "indigenization" of social sci-ence research in the developing countries is an up-hill task and calls for a concerted action of all the parties concerned. There is hardly any need to stress that the efforts of Unesco, social science non-governmental organizations and regional institutions, far from overlapping, are naturally complementary.

Here are some instances of joint activities in this field. The International Social Science Council (ISSC), a leading social science non-governmental organization, was involved in preparing the ground for Unesco's new regional programme for Africa. It was entrusted with the task of preparing, with the help of a group of consultants and specialists from various African countries, a working docu-ment on African needs in the social science field and proposing research themes which could later

be adopted by African teams carrying out multi-national comparative research. The document in question, "The situation and perspectives of so-cial science in tropical and equatorial Africa" constituted a basis for a Unesco round table in Lomé in 1972, where research priorities (urbani-zation and rural development) were finally adopted by the African social scientists themselves.

In the case of Asia, mention should be made of AASSREC (Asian Association of Social Science Research Councils). Helping in the building up of national councils (usually an emanation of govern-mental policies - a pertinent consideration for Unesco as an intergovernmental organization) and relating their activities to wider collaborative arrangements within and between major regions has been among the aims of Unesco over the last decade or so. This is particularly true of Asia, where well established and active councils are in existence in many countries and are dynamic factors in the development of social science re-search, nationally and regionally. An Asian Association of Social Science Research Councils (AASSREC) was launched at the Asian Conference on Social Science Teaching and Research organized with Unesco's support by the Indian Social Science Council in Simla in 1973. Several research pri-orities were distinguished by the meeting and served as a basis for further deliberations. Rep-resentatives of AASSREC as well as a number of scholars who hold responsible positions and/or are personally active in national social science councils took part in the Symposium on Social Research Development in Asia which Unesco organized subsequently in Kopo in 1974, and which advised on the choice of regional research projects (the rôle of a university in national development, and modern professions) to be initiated and carried out under the Organization's auspices.

10. But certain weaknesses relating to action for the benefit of "indigenization" of social science research must be recognized.

On the part of the countries and regions con-cerned and their own social science institutions, which by the very nature are to be the main carriers and promotors of "indigenization", there is a marked paucity of basic facilities and qualified social scientists who could be engaged in research. The traditional university structure is ill adapted to research (in the developing countries, most re-search centres and institutes are located in higher educational establishments) which by and large, receives insufficient backing from governments except for very immediate and practical purposes. Communcation between social scientists both within a given country (except the very smallest) and -even more so - at the regional level is poor (in a region like Africa this is coupled with rather poor communication between the English-speaking and French-speaking countries) while "corridor" re-lationships with Europe and the United States still very much prevail. There is a lack of continuity of certain activities as regards both research projects themselves and staff involved even within the same research centres.

On the part of the social science non-governmental organizations, their inadequate geographical reach is a recognized weakness. Most of them, owing to the historical circumstances in which the social science developed, are located in Europe and North America and because of this they draw mainly upon local intellectual resources; most social science meetings are organized in these two regions; and the research themes are related to a large extent to European or American problems. Although serious efforts have already been made by various associations to improve the existing situation, there is still a long way to go to arrive at a true internationalization of the work of the social science community. Various illustrations of means that might be used to overcome these difficulties have been frequently suggested, including the associating of Third World scholars and their institutions actively and effectively in the planning, execution and evaluation of the programme of the respective associations; holding more meetings, symposia and congresses outside the developed "North"; involving Third World scholars in collaborative schemes with regard to research, training, documentation and dissemination of publications, on a basis of genuine partnership, etc. The federative structure of the International Social Science Council, the adoption of which Unesco helped to bring about, should make it possible, among other advantages, to promote the participation by scholars of the Third World in the international life of the social sciences.

On the part of Unesco itself, it is the slenderness of resources for the development of social science research in the Third World. Funds available under the Regular Programme are barely sufficient to provide for the stimulation and initiation of research at the regional level. Fully-fledged and long-term research activities would require extra-budgetary funds. The creation of social science co-ordination centres in Africa and in the Arab region, and the appointment of a social science adviser for Asia, will yield a framework and machinery for this action, but again on the condition that extra-budgetary sources, in particular from UNDP, would be forthcoming. Unfortunately, except for projects in Latin America, social science regional programmes submitted to UNDP have not met with a positive reception. Patient work by the Secretariat will therefore be required to persuade the major funding agencies that projects dealing with social science research are well worth their support; that even if the contribution of the social sciences may not be immediately apparent it will be essential to development in the long run; that as yet disappointing results obtained through international action on behalf of development may be due to the fact that competent international organizations have still not taken the human factor sufficiently

into account; or at least that they have in too many cases underestimated the complexity of the socio-cultural factors involved and unwisely excluded from the field of operations anything that might run counter to a short-term view of effectiveness, but have in so doing actually reduced the effectiveness of projects.

A vital rôle in this respect can be played by the international associations in general and by social scientists in the developing countries in particular, by their national branches of international associations and national social science research councils (if already in existence). They can help make their governments fully aware of the importance of social science research and of the significance of the regional framework, which in turn might persuade possible international donors of the potentialities of action at the regional and national levels.

III

11. Three major types of social science research can be distinguished: (i) basic or fundamental research, concerned with the advancement of knowledge per se; (ii) applied research, concerned with practical application of knowledge which seeks to be immediately translated into action; (iii) problem-oriented research, lying between the previous two types, concerned with providing new types of information, the clarification of alternatives and widened perspectives in what is considered as major problems in the life of a society. This distinction, convenient as it may be, should not however be strained too far, considering that the differences may sometimes be merely a matter of degree. Basic, so-called theoretical, research may lead to useful applications, while applied research may open up new avenues for basic research. Applied as well as basic research may in certain cases prove to be stimulating and enriching for problem-focused research. Although in applied research the progression from study to action is normally shorter and more perceptible, and effectiveness of results is better assured, these elements are not alien to the problem-oriented research; together with the provision of useful ways of diagnosing social situations, it aims ultimately at estimating the effects of social action - not only of past events but also of alternative or preferred causes of action, all this of great value for the decision-making process and administration.

How does Unesco's work fit into the above-mentioned framework?

12. One of the main concerns of Unesco is the promotion of knowledge. Consequently, the Organization has shown from the very beginning a very active interest in various aspects of basic social science research, such as: description and definition of terms and concepts of fundamental

importance in the social sciences; improvement of the methodology of comparative international and cultural research; promotion of interdisciplinary studies both in study of man and society, and between social and natural sciences; the uses of quantitative methods in the social sciences; clarification of concepts and criteria relating to the universal vocation and regional roots of the social sciences. To further these aims Unesco has been organizing many meetings and symposia with a view to assessing the existing situation, bringing together the various strands of the discussion and clearing the ground for the preparation of relevant studies to be undertaken under Unesco's auspices. The overall objective has been to create a universal scientific language and universal principles of a nature to render different scientific propositions translatable and acceptable by the communis opinio doctorum.

Many studies, both in the past and at present, bear out Unesco's interest in basic social science research. Among them are "A dictionary of the social sciences" (published in English in 1964, in Arabic in 1967, and in Spanish in 1975); a similar work is now being prepared on Portuguese terminology, "Handbook for social research in urban areas" (1965); "Main trends of research in the social and human sciences" (the first volume appeared in 1970, the second volume is in press); "Race, science and society" (a revised edition of the previously published collection of essays and statements on race and racial prejudice; the French edition appeared in 1974, the English edition is in print); the collection of texts on administrative management for development (the French edition appeared in 1974, the English edition will be published in 1976); "Sociological theories and race" (an interdisciplinary international expert meeting will be held on this subject in 1976; the proceedings will be published); "New trends in formalization in the social sciences" (forthcoming); "Mathematical models in international relations" (forthcoming).

A basic question to be asked here is to what extent Unesco's endeavours in the field of basic research are relevant to the specific needs and postulates of the developing countries, as expressed by the "regionalization" movement. The latter, as is known, does not reject the social sciences as they exist in the West, but does take a critical stance towards their ethnocentrism, emphasizing their cultural biases and criticizing their sometimes completely unfounded universalistic pretentions. The twin concern for Unesco in the realm of basic social science research is therefore to ensure that (i) the demands of the developing countries are fully met; (ii) at the same time, to promote regionalization, rather than the splitting of the social sciences into mutually incompatible schools. This approach constitutes an enrichment and a step towards universalization thanks to the contributions from different cultural and socio-political spheres. Examination of this important problem is envisaged in 18 C/5.

13. Most Unesco-sponsored research in the developing countries is problem-oriented; it seems in fact that what is sometimes labelled as applied research belongs really to the problem-oriented type. Such research carried out by or under the auspices of Unesco can be roughly divided into two categories: (i) empirical field research; (ii) non-field investigation.

The aim of the first type of research is to state in definable and measurable terms the nature of the relationship between phenomena in such a way that this relationship can be (i) empirically tested; (ii) variation in one phenomenon (an independent variable) can be used to explain variation in another phenomenon (a dependent variable). This involves all the necessary elements of contemporary social science research: the identification of indicators; construction of measurement tools; elaboration of methods and procedure for sampling and control of the collection of data; data collection; the analysis and interpretation of findings. The actual research may be of a rather simple ex-post-facto nature or, of a more sophisticated experimental character involving data collection at three points in time (baseline, interim, terminal) and the introduction of both experimental and control groups. It may satisfy itself with establishing the relationship between the two variables or, try to assess the effect, of a third or more intervening variables in the framework of a multi-variate analysis. Whatever the case may be, this type of problem-oriented research is based upon original data gathered in a field study (regional research projects in Asia and Africa, studies on race and ethnic problems are examples).

The other type of research is based entirely upon documentary sources. Sound research studies can be developed from the materials already published and available in library and archives collections: demographic studies based on population statistics gathered and published by various agencies, which serve as the raw data for analysis of a specific problem; the analysis of the characteristics of the content of communication in a given field; reports on the curricula, methods and conditions of teaching in social science disciplines; country surveys on national resources and facilities in social science research, teaching and data sources; reports on trends in recent research on a given problem combined with an annotated bibliography; the synthesis of the findings of research studies, which draws upon the research of several disciplines and relates them to the same social phenomenon; studies on objectives, criteria, methods, mechanisms and procedures relating to development efforts at the national and regional levels, etc. Current research in Unesco is predominently of this type.

14. The importance given to applied (action-oriented) research, always a characteristic feature

of Unesco's activities in the developing countries, was further stressed by the establishment in the biennium 1971-1972 of a new unit responsible for the elaboration and spread of social science methods and analysis which have to be applied in the planning, programming and evaluation of development activities. This programme, which deals with simulation models, evaluation techniques, and indicators of socio-economic change, began to move in the last biennium from the professional or technical level, to that of practical application, by making these methods available and accessible to government planners.

IV

15. Before giving an account of Unesco's research in the developing countries, mention should be made of the specific situation in which the Organization finds itself with respect to social science research.

(i) Unesco is not a research institution, its rôle is rather that of sponsor and manager of research projects. Once the research priorities are selected and defined in the C/5 document, the field of available expertise is canvassed and participation of local scholars and institutions sought. Research projects are assigned to the latter under contract. With regard to the degree of articulation of research priorities - which are our main concern - there can be, roughly speaking, two models: one when the research priorities are worked out and defined within the Organization (this may, of course, imply various sources of inspiration); and the other, when only the research "perspective" is outlined leaving the actual definition of priorities to research utilizers (Member States) and/or researchers themselves. As regards the execution of research projects, Unesco's rôle may be more pronounced and comprise, for instance, preparation of guidelines, research design, evaluation of interim and final reports, editing of manuscripts for publication, etc. or be restricted to only a few areas of involvement.

(ii) Unesco's research is designed to bring about multiplier or demonstration effects. It serves to stimulate, encourage, direct, national and regional efforts which will subsequently function on their own momentum.

(iii) Unesco's programme is selective in character. It aims at promoting social science research on certain problems which are of prime importance to Member States and the world community as a whole, as they affect Unesco's fields of competence. In other words, the Organization strives to have a limited but significant research programme.

(iv) Unesco's budget for social science research is relatively small; in fact it is no more than "seed money". The Organization cannot compete with many public or private bodies active in

this field in the developing countries. However, Unesco's social science programme has a greater impact than its financial limits might indicate. "The rôle of Unesco is more important for the opportunities it provides as broker, mediator and stimulator than for the size of its budget."[1] Unesco's world-wide scope and intergovernmental character, combined with access, within the framework of international intellectual co-operation, to direct scholarly and scientific participation, help provide a framework for collaborative schemes that frequently can be arranged through no other channel.

16. What follows is an account of Unesco's research activities in the developing countries in the biennia 1973-1974 and 1975-1976. It should be stressed that each research project is in some way unique; each has its own history, internal dynamics and characteristic features, particularly with respect to how priorities have been established and research conducted. An attempt will be made to reveal the specificity of the respective projects.

(i) Regional interdisciplinary research in Asia

As mentioned earlier, a Unesco symposium on social science research development in Asia was held in Jakarta-Kopo (Indonesia), in February 1974, with 17 participants from 16 countries in the Asian region. On the basis of its recommendations, two multinational and multidisciplinary research teams, each led by a co-ordinator, were established on "Modern occupations and development" and "The rôle of the university in national development" respectively. In accordance with the principle of "indigenization", research priorities were established on the spot by the Asian social scientists themselves; the research teams were recruited in the region concerned; meetings of research teams to discuss methodology and interim results were envisaged to be held in situ.

The study raises the problem of the feasibility of comparison, one which besets all cross-cultural, cross-social and cross-national research. The first problem is comparability of data. This may be possible to ensure through the use of a common basic framework of concepts and tools. However, the Asian countries belong to many different levels of development. The relation of each set of data to its socio-cultural and economic context may remain so specific as to make a comparison of the findings, and the formulation of any policy recommendations, an extremely difficult task. Therefore, the scope of comparison needs to be carefully determined in terms of the countries involved. To ensure maximum comparability of the data collected, consultation is envisaged

(1) Gene M. Lyons, Globalizing the Social Sciences, "Political Science", Vol. VI, No. 1, Winter, 1973, page 3.

between the principal investigators at the stages of: research design formulation; mid-course appraisal; and preparation of draft reports.

(a) Modern occupations and development

This is obviously a research subject of great importance. The emergence of modern occupations and professions is closely interwoven with the process of modernization which calls for trained manpower development. The study is concentrating in its first stage on the medical profession - health conditions are intimately linked with almost every aspect of economic activity and social life in general. This study will constitute a model for further research on what can be called "hard" professions with respect to the development and modernization efforts, i.e. scientists and engineers. Five Asian countries (Afghanistan, India, Iran, Malaysia, and Sri Lanka) and two social science disciplines (sociology and political science) are represented in the study. The inquiries will be exploratory, analytical, and diagnostic in scope, i.e. they will aim to describe the prevailing situation, to analyse this situation in terms of correlations and causative factors and so make some forecasts about the growth of this service in the foreseeable future. The following areas are investigated: social background of the physicians; reasons for choice of the profession; medical education and rôle perception; professional work environment; rôle performance; life style; social responsibility; relations with practitioners of traditional medicine; patients' view of the physicians; self-assessment by the physicians.
Research period: 1974-1976. Research funds: $28,000.

(b) The rôle of the university in national development

The problems involved can be formulated as the following questions: What are the structure, the external milieux and key functions of the university? How can university education best be used as a means of social restructuring and redefinition of socio-economic rôles? What is the effect of different types of university education on social stratification and social mobility; on the formation of modern élite and entrepreneurship as carriers and promoters of development; attitudes, motives and incentives with respect to social change, technological progress, inventions, innovation and imitation? What are the possibilities of involving university teachers and students in development efforts? Five countries of the region (Indonesia, Republic of Korea, Pakistan, the Philippines, Thailand) and four disciplines (sociology, economics, political science, public administration) are represented in the inquiry.
Research period: 1974-1976. Research funds: $28,000.

(ii) Regional interdisciplinary research in Africa

A search for a new approach to social science research in this region began in the biennium 1971-1972. It was in this context that a Unesco round table on regional social science activities in Africa south of the Sahara, held in Lomé (Togo) in October 1972, recommended to undertake research in urbanization and rural development, considered to be priority fields in Africa. The Lomé meeting also emphasized that research in these areas had to be conceived within the framework of national and regional development planning, and that in order to contribute effectively to national development efforts in Africa, social science research should adopt an interdisciplinary, comparative cross-national and problem-oriented approach. A subsequent symposium on social science co-operation in Africa south of the Sahara, held in Dar es Salaam (Tanzania) in December 1973, spelt out in more detail the theoretical and methodological framework of the study as well as defined research topics in each of the two large themes. Following the recommendations and discussions of the two meetings, two multinational, interdisciplinary research teams, recruited in the region concerned, were set up to work on the themes selected. It should be stressed that the researchers come from and the research itself is concluded in, both anglophone and francophone countries. Social science research in Africa under Unesco's auspices is therefore an instrument of overcoming the existing socio-cultural differences. In contrast to the Asian study, where each national project deals with the same problems within a larger theme (occupation or university respectively), each of the national projects in Africa is concentrating on a specific problem within the general framework provided by urbanization or rural development respectively. Comparability of data will be ensured only with regard to the general aspects of each of these two themes. The African research, which in 1974 was carried out directly under Unesco's auspices, became since 1975 the responsibility of the newly established Centre for the Co-ordination of Social Science Research and Documentation in Africa south of the Sahara (CERDAS).

(a) Urbanization

The particular projects are dealing with: (1) Land use, housing and social problems (Tanzania). This project looks at the relationship between policy, planning, land use, housing and the effects of these on the urban population, particularly on social problems. (2) Urban-rural organizational links (Ethiopia). Voluntary organizations (some with multi-purpose functions), which cut across and do not recognize the rural-urban dichtomy, are studied in a pre-colonial, non-industrialized city.

(3) African town life and cultural personality (Ivory Coast). The study examines the dominant cultural models in contemporary urban Africa: traditional, foreign or new African ones. (4) Urban study of Zaire. The subject of study is the relationship between the capital city and its hinterland.

Research period: 1974-1976. Research funds: $50,000.

(b) Rural development

The projects in question are on: (1) Informal education of rural youth with a view to integrated local development (Cameroon). This project will ultimately help rural youth organize itself to fully utilize local resources, and to elaborate instruments useful both to rural development and to the constitution of elements for the reform of primary education programmes. (2) Rural development problems in the Kiva (Zaire). This is a study of functional relationships between urban and rural agglomerations in the region. (3) Problems of the arid zones (Kenya). The study concentrates on methods of adjustment of the population to the conditions caused by the drought, population movements, the introduction of adequate technology and alternative strategies for increased production. (4) Reorganization of rural society for development: the case of the Ujaama villages (Tanzania). A study of socio-economic organization of these villages and of their transformation into self-reliant production units and rural communities in general.

Research period: 1974-1976. Research funds: $50,000.

(iii) Community development

The Korean National Commission for Unesco sponsored an International Seminar on the Comparative Study of Community Development in December 1973. In pursuance of the resolutions of the seminar, the Commission proposed comparative research on this theme in four countries, India, Korea, Tanzania and Yugoslavia and requested Unesco to act as the executing agency under the fund-in-trust scheme. The basic objectives of the study are: (a) to assess the feasibility of community development models suitable for the developing countries, with special reference to the environmental and political context of each country; (b) to help establish studies in community development as an academic discipline. Although specific research design and requirements of material must be tailored to fit each country's need, a basis for comparability among all the country surveys is also sought.

Research period: 1975-1976. Research funds: $56,000.

(iv) Racialism, colonialism and apartheid

This long-standing project, which forms an integral part of a wider concern of the Organization, i.e. human rights and problems of peace, enables one to gain an insight into how the idea of comparative research in this important and highly value-loaded field has evolved, how the priorities have been established, and what approaches and methods have been employed in the conduct of research.

The Secretariat is asked by various General Conference resolutions and by United Nations resolutions (e.g. resolution 10.1 concerning Unesco's contribution to peace and its tasks with respect to the elimination of colonialism and racialism, adopted by the seventeenth session, and the United Nations Decade for Action to Combat Racism and Racial Discrimination launched in 1974) to have as one of its objectives the study of the cause and results of racial discrimination and apartheid. This sets the general framework for the series of studies.

The first push in the programme in the field in the early sixties was for the popularization of "scientific facts on race". This was in line with the idea that knowledge of certain biological facts would end social discrimination. At this level no research is needed, only the popularization of research already done. The slant of the programme and its widening to include research was the result of several factors. The swing from considering racism as a question of simple morality or ignorance to studying racism and racial discrimination as structurally determined and therefore a proper subject for study by other social disciplines, mainly history, sociology, social anthropology and social psychology. However, here other problems arose. The first had to do with lack of comparative material. Most studies on race were concentrated on black-white relationships in the United States of America. The second problem had to do with the very definition "social" race in terms of social structure as distinct from ethnicity or class. The third problem was the operation of key social institutions, e.g. education, the mass media, in societies where race was important. But perhaps the most important decision as to priorities within the race programme came from the debate carried on, not by the social scientists, but by the underprivileged themselves who challenged the concept of the applicability of the notion of the pluralist society in societies of deep seated cleavage as well as the automatic nature of class consciousness. It became obvious that the theoretical models used needed to be reassessed and if necessary modified by the concrete analysis of situations chosen carefully for their theoretical importance as well as for their social relevance.

The method of conducting research could differ considerably. One example of this is the series of studies on ethnicity in Latin America and the Caribbean. For the Caribbean three approaches were adopted: a contract was signed with a local institution for two country studies; a researcher who was in the area was asked to supplement this with an ethnic component built into his research on community development, and a theoretical paper was commissioned to a Caribbean who had done work on class in Britain. For Latin America the approaches were also quite different. In the case of Mexico, the Mexican Government already has a major project in the Mezquital on the development of rural Indian areas. "Seed money" was given to the University of Mexico to build into this major government project a component on ethnicity. In the case of Bolivia and Chile a contract was signed with FLACSO. This permitted graduate students to work on relevant issues under the guidance of one of the lecturers at FLACSO. These studies were also used to reassess certain theories, e.g. "plural society" as reinterpreted by Caribbean scholars, the theory of dependency, etc., and encourage co-operative research between the English-speaking Caribbean and Latin America. The same sort of procedure was applied to Asian studies, but in addition a meeting was organized (Nepal, November 1974) which brought social scientists of the host country in working contact with Asian scholars and also provided for an exchange of information between the researchers in Latin America and the Caribbean on the one hand and Asia and New Zealand on the other.

It is therefore hoped by these area studies to contribute to the general advancement of social science theory, to encourage regional co-operation and to finance - within the limited funds available - post-graduate research on relevant issues.

Unesco is to some extent hampered, however, by the very success of the programme. It is one of the few organizations that has done comparative research in this area over a long period of time and is therefore called upon by various other organizations to provide money and technical and academic assistance (both in short supply) in setting up their own programmes.

(a) Trends in ethnic group relations

After completion in 1972 of a first series of studies in three African countries, field investigations on ethnic group relations have been made since 1973 in selected Latin American and Caribbean countries (Bolivia, Chile, Mexico, the English-speaking Caribbean). This project has raised several important issues: social stratification in a colonial society; the theory of dependency; race and class; the theory of the plural society and enclave cultures. The results of the studies will be published this year in English and Spanish.

Similar studies began in 1973-1974 on ethnic group relations in a selected number of Asian and Oceanic countries (India, Nepal, the Philippines, New Zealand). The work will be continued on problems such as the relationships between linguistic and religious conflicts and industrial development; social mobility in urban areas; the interaction between majority and minority cultures;

relationships between social stratification within a group and general social stratification; social relations among ethnic groups in areas of resettlement; and the particular situation of minority groups specializing in trading activities. The results of these studies will be evaluated by groups of consultants and published in 1977-1978.

Research period: 1973-1976. Research funds: $117,685.

(b) The effects of racial policies in Rhodesia, Namibia and the Portuguese territories

In the series of studies initiated in 1971-1972 as a continuation of work done on South Africa, on the effects of racial policies on education, science, culture and information in the above-mentioned countries, work has been done on the effects of Rhodesian policy on education, science, culture and information. It deals with European settlement in Rhodesia; the growth of a discriminatory structure in education; the effect of legislation on African culture and institutions; and the resultant dual society under white control. A similar book on the effects of apartheid on human rights in education, science, culture and information is being prepared on Namibia. The publication on Portuguese territories appeared in 1974 ("Portuguese colonialism in Africa: the end of an era"). It surveys the history of Portuguese colonialism in Africa and the structure of the society, analyses the reforms of the 1960s and considers the effect of the Portuguese colonies on southern Africa.

Research period: 1971-1976. Research funds (for 1973-1976): $33,580.

(v) Social science research in development

The major aims of the programme are (a) to encourage university social science teaching and research to respond to the needs of development planning and management, and to stimulate the use by governments of social science research in planning, and (b) to review and assess the progress of the United Nations Second Development Decade (which puts more stress on social objectives than did the First Decade) in Unesco's field of competence.

Description of relevant research projects, both of field and library type, will be given below. Here mention will be made of meetings of specialists - a typical Unesco activity - dealing with specific aspects of the problem under review. These meetings clearly constitute a borderline case. In terms of consciously perceived aims, they usually do not fall into the category of research. But they normally give, through the working papers that constitute a basis for discussions, a critical review of existing research and open up new perspectives for further investigations. So much so, the problem of development planning and the rôle which the social sciences can play therein, where studied by two regional meetings held in Asia (Bangkok, May 1972) and Africa (Nairobi, December 1974) respectively. The first meeting was dealing with what may be called "technical" problems - methods and approaches such as methods of systems analysis, simulation models and evaluation techniques; the second meeting was characterized by an integrated overall approach and this in two senses (a) theory and practice in development planning were regarded as an interacting system; (b) the symposium was interdisciplinary in the widest sense of the word bringing together professionals from various social sciences disciplines. Both meetings came up with recommendations concerning the measures to be adopted to encourage research and training in this field and to establish links between research workers and planners.

There is no doubt that Unesco's priorities in this field are to a large extent a response to resolution No. 2626 (XXV) on International Development Strategy for the Second United Nations Development Decade. On the other hand, Unesco's concern for the social problems of development is a long-standing one and this innovative activity therefore does not represent a break with the past but is rooted in experience already acquired.

(a) Monographs on the application of social sciences to development

They highlight the characteristics of the countries selected (Asia, Africa and Latin America are involved) and, particularly, the disparities in the level of development from the economic, social and cultural points of view. Comparisons are made with a view to designing a system of reference for use in analysing specific situations and making it possible to adopt development aid programmes more closely to local conditions, in particular in Unesco's fields of competence.

In 1974, three studies were prepared on the social and cultural factors of development in Cameroon, Ecuador and Venezuela respectively. As regards the method employed in selecting research institutions to which the studies could be commissioned, a consultant undertook a mission of one month to each country, and made contact with local institutions which were recommended to him by the National Commission. For 1975, three more contracts are under preparation. It is likely that one Asian, one African and another Latin American country will be chosen.
Research period: 1973-1976. Research funds: $30,000.

(b) Aid to development

In 1975-1976, objectives, criteria, methods, mechanisms and procedures of development aid in the field of Unesco's competence will be examined in the light of past experience. A preliminary study will be undertaken by two senior consultants. Subsequently a consultative committee of experts will meet to study, in the light of the results of this work, the problems and difficulties which hinder development aid operations and propose such reappraisals as may appear necessary in the approach to aid programmes and the procedures for implementing them. On the basis of the conclusions of this committee, a report will be presented first to the Executive Board and then to the nineteenth session of the General Conference.
Research period: 1975-1976. Research funds: $44,200.

(c) Unified approach to development

Studies will be carried out for the purpose of analysing and evaluating a cross-section of the experiments carried out in a number of countries; reviewing the research which has been done on the "unified approach to development" by the United Nations, the Specialized Agencies and the institutes of the United Nations system and by scientific research institutions; drawing conclusions from this research and assessing its relevance to the planning of activities of the various sectors of Unesco and to their needs for concepts and tools. Particular attention will be given to the relationship between development and social justice and to the conditions to be fulfilled if development is to be well balanced from the economic, social and cultural points of view.
Research period: 1975-1976. Research funds: $33,200.

(vi) Social science studies on population questions

The activities described under this heading are part of an inter-sectoral programme in the field of population. The purpose of this programme, largely financed by the United Nations Fund for Population Activities (UNFPA), is to improve knowledge and increase awareness of the causes and consequences of population change, of their interrelationships with other aspects of social, cultural and economic change and development, and ultimately of their implications for human rights and the quality of life.

Despite significant advances made in social science research in the field of population, major deficiencies in knowledge still remain on the relative impact of social, cultural and economic factors and of structural social institutions on demographic behaviour. Unesco has thus focused its research activities in this field on interdisciplinary studies on selective social and cultural aspects of the interrelations between demographic change and socio-economic development, particularly at the family level.

Family sociological research with emphasis on fertility behaviour, begun in 1973 under the Regular Budget, continued with the development of research studies in the Arab States. The problems studied within the area of the family and social change were selected in consultation with the national researchers themselves. Methodologically, the studies were intended to be exploratory, utilizing in-depth, open-ended interview or participant-observation techniques based on individualistic study designs and very small samples, seeking an understanding of a wide variety of factors determining how families adapt to social changes. Consequently they were neither easily generalizable on a national level nor comparable at an international, cross-cultural level.

At a workshop of co-operating institutes and research workers from the Arab States and Turkey, convened in Beirut in 1974 to discuss methodological problems involved in studies of the adjustment of families to social change, most participants felt the need for studies with larger samples and more structural interview schedules, as well as for the development of comparative cross-national surveys. The World Population Conference at Bucharest in August 1974 was a major event which took new directions for population problems and research connected therewith very much in line with the Organization's own control proposals and preoccupations. A proposal for research along the lines mentioned above, to be financed by UNFPA as of 1976, is in preparation.

(a) Family studies

Three studies of family adjustment to social change in urban situations, with emphasis on changing fertility patterns, were begun in 1974 in collaboration with research institutes and universities in Jordan (Aman), Morocco (Rabat) and Iran (Tabriz). Reports are expected in 1975. Two more studies concerning Egypt and the United Arab Emirates are being commissioned. A meeting will be held in Tehran in 1976 in collaboration with the Organization for the Promotion of Social Sciences in the Middle East, on "Family, kinship and social, change". A novel approach to comparative, international studies of changing family structures and functions will be discussed and the conclusions of previous family studies, with special attention to those supported through Unesco's special science research programme, will be presented.

Research period: 1973-1976. Research funds: $24,000.

(b) Studies on population action programmes and the values of cultures

The aim of these studies is to explore the influence of societal cultural systems and the rôle of various "subcultures" within societies as they impinge upon the individual cultural traits that are related to demographic behaviour, especially in relation to family-size preferences and the practice of contraception. Studies in Nigeria, Pakistan, the Philippines and Thailand are envisaged. Contacts were made with the Committee for International Co-ordination of National Research in Demography for identification of appropriate national institutions that would carry out the research. These research activities are of further relevance in the context of International Women's Year since they are also concerned with the relationship between demographic behaviour and the status of women in the family and in society, and the cultural norms and values related to sex rôles.

Research period: 1975-1976. Research funds: $24,000.

(vii) Quality of the environment

The social science research in the field of environment is part of the integrated Unesco environment programme, whose main component is a long-term intergovernmental programme on "Man and the Biosphere" (MAB). It has been recognized from the very beginning that MAB projects need to be planned and carried out as interdisciplinary efforts with full co-operation of physical, biological and social scientists. The results of the 1972 Stockholm Conference push that objective further by recognizing that problems of environment need to be reviewed and dealt with in the context of social change and social development. The work relating to the specifically human aspects of the environment and human settlements in particular, was given in Unesco a decisive impetus in 1974 by the establishment of a co-ordination unit "Man in his environment - human settlements". This is the context in which social sciences priorities in the field of environment have been established. The overall concept underlying all social science investigations is that of quality of life, particularly in human settlements. More specifically, the projects are to deal with: the way environment is perceived, whether by children or adults; the understanding by decision-makers of the consequences of their own decisions in environmental matters; the effects of tourism on social and cultural life; the involvement of the general public in environmental matters; the informed awareness of the ethics of environment and the implementation of human rights in matters of environment; the participation and interaction by citizens in environmental policies; the contribution of the social sciences to the better planning of the human settlements.

(a) Perception of environmental quality

The study begun in 1973 of children's perception of their immediate environment, was completed in 1974. Out of three countries involved, one was a developing country (Argentina, the other two being Australia and Poland). The main objective of the local surveys, carried out in marginal urban areas, was to establish the way in which children perceive, use and react to their environment. This field work sought also to bring out the way in which teachers and official bodies may benefit from the results obtained so as to evolve a setting which children will find more satisfying. Lastly, the project helped to spread the knowledge and the use of research techniques which make it possible to study the mechanisms involved in overall perception of the environment. In 1975-1976, this project will be extended to other age groups and social strata and to many different types of country, especially in the developing regions, and type of environment - both urban and rural. These studies aim at isolating significant indicators of the processes of perception and at providing guidance for planners, educators and social workers. They will be designed so as to make inter-regional comparisons possible at a later stage.

Research period: 1973-1976. Research funds: $29,000.

(b) The effects of tourism

The study of the effect of tourism on the social, economic, and cultural life and on the physical environment of the Island of Bali, Indonesia was conducted in 1973-1975 by the research teams of the local University of Udayana. The research revealed the negative impact of mass tourism on the biological (of unique value), man-made and social environments of the Island due to the large numbers of people involved, their superficial, anonymous and irresponsible attitude towards both the physical and social environment and the ill effects of the search for profits on the inherent values and way of life of the local community. This project is conceived as a pilot project which could be extended to other countries in the region.

Research period: 1973-1975. Research funds: $9,000.

(c) Environmental programming exercise

This pilot project, put in operation in 1973, was a practical simulation exercise using modern techniques and methods (modelling procedures, use of computers, application of games theory, etc.) and was designed to provide a group of government planners from various regions with the opportunity to examine the consequences of a series of economic and social decisions on the environment and the way in which these modifications of the immediate environment would be perceived and felt (often in unexpected ways) by the public, at the same time increasing their awareness of the importance of environment problems. The subject chosen dealt with the effect on environment of the expansion of tourism and the facilities which it

involved. The Bariloche Foundation (Argentina) prepared the plan for this exercise and this was subjected to a test in 1974. Another demonstration took place at the European Centre for the Co-ordination of Research and Documentation in the Social Sciences (Vienna). It should be mentioned that the results are being utilized in the management of environment of the local community.

Research period: 1973-1974. Research funds: $13,500.

(d) Public participation in environmental decisions

This project, launched in 1973, is concerned with the testing, evaluation and improvement of new techniques and new methods of teaching designed to increase public awareness (among students and adults) of environment problems and public understanding of the way in which the environment is affected by social decisions and behaviour, and to encourage active public participation in a well-defined and coherent environment policy. Studies on methods for ensuring the participation of the public in environmental decision-making were completed in three different settings, one of them being a developing country undergoing rapid change (Brazil, the other two were Canada and Italy). This project is being continued in 1975-1976; it will be carried out in even more widely differing geographical, economic and social contexts, so as to enable a final comparative analysis. To this end, regional research guides will be designed, especially for the developing regions.

Research period: 1973-1976. Research funds: $35,200.

(e) Social and cultural consequences of environmental changes

As a major social science contribution to the "Man and the Biosphere" programme, research will be focused in 1975-1976 on the interdependence of the socio-cultural and environmental consequences of development plans in specific areas in the developing world, taking account of factors connected with the depletion of natural resources. To this end, studies will be made on possible changes in the cultural identity, values and norms of the societies concerned, with the aim of analysing how development plans can be implemented without causing unnecessary social harm. For field investigation, tropical forest areas were selected in Latin America, West Africa and Asia.

Research period: 1975-1976. Research funds: $16,000.

(viii) Youth in contemporary society

If the attitudes and viewpoints adopted by young people regarding current social and international problems are to be correctly interpreted, the place of young people in society must be understood from the sociological and psycho-sociological standpoints. The activities of the Youth Division, which serves as a focal point for all programmes concerning young people, must therefore rely heavily on social science findings. Comparative research was conducted in 1973-1974 on specific problems of young people in four different regions of the world, three of them being developing regions. The three studies in question were dealing respectively with: (a) the problem of the university and the place and rôle of students in society in Latin America (countries involved: Argentina, Chile, Peru, Uruguay and Venezuela); (b) the problem of the vocational training of young people in Arab States; (c) the problem of the exodus of rural youth in the Indian sub-continent (Bangladesh, India, Pakistan and Sri Lanka).

The studies were characterized by the following features: young people were given opportunities of expressing themselves and threshing out their ideas, doubts and problems together; the ideas and reactions of youth led to the reappraisal of a certain number of postulates underlying current research; young people were studied not as "objects" but considered as "subjects" and partners (for instance, the research problems were posed by themselves).

Research period: 1973-1974. Research funds: $27,595.

(ix) Drug abuse

A series of studies and surveys have been undertaken in order to identify the set of socio-cultural factors that determine drug-taking, with special emphasis, in developing countries, on aspects such as rapid urbanization, disruption of social communication, etc.

Research period: 1973-1976. Research funds: $18,000.

(x) Methods for the application of the social sciences

Activities in this field involve a research component which may be original, but which remains derivative in relation to current creative work in the social sciences throughout the world, and is strictly subordinated to practical requirements. The studies are not however purely formal: far from being merely an arrangement of elements, they entail an effort to work out and systematize specific social realities in terms of the objectives of international action, which confers on them the quality of genuine social science studies. The instruments and procedures thus devised in close consultation with the "users" are designed to be applied by the latter, or under their supervision, in such a way as to meet their project requirements, particularly in regard to planning and evaluation. The practical experience thus acquired in turn leads either to

refine or adjust these intellectual tools, or to extend their application to new fields where methodological innovation is needed, or else to turn back to the social science for fresh light thrown by recent research.

Research activities fall under the three main headings corresponding to the areas of interest of the division concerned: social indicators, simulation models and evaluation.

(a) Social indicators

Earlier work in this field concentrated upon defining concepts and developing mathematical methods for indicator selection. This work led to a broadening of human resources analysis to include investigation of the interrelations between human resources and economic development. A turning point was the shift in emphasis from a comparison between countries to a detailed review of indicators within countries. A series of national country studies was completed in 1973-1974 (out of four studies, three concerned the developing countries, i.e. Kenya, Venezuela and Zambia, the fourth one being Yugoslavia). Under the project "Applicability of social indicators to development planning", four research studies are foreseen in 1975. A research study will be carried out in Sudan on disparities of development, in relation to the different socio-economic groups and to the different geographical areas of the country. Two similar studies are being carried out, in Asia, one in the Philippines and the other in Thailand. The studies will describe the within-country development context, emphasizing particularly the spatial pattern at national and provincial levels. They will be discussed in December 1975 in a workshop grouping development planners of the two countries and held in co-operation with their Unesco National Commissions. Research on the same subject will be carried out in Kenya, again stressing disparities in development on both the social and geographical planes. The contractor will be the local University of Nairobi. The research will be the basis of a demonstration study for discussion in a workshop in 1976, grouping a number of Kenyan planners in Nairobi.

A new directive on the work on the development of systems of social indicators is research on indicators on quality of life and of the environment. This work which has just started will contribute, at a first stage, to environment aspects of development planning. It is anticipated that close collaboration with national institutes will be sought, as has been the case with other aspects of the work on social indicators, as described above.

Research period: 1973-1976. Research funds: $49,700.

(b) Simulation models

In addition to the adaptation and application of the Unesco Educational Simulation Model in a number of developing countries (Kenya, Sudan, Saudi Arabia, Philippines) a research project to adapt and use the model to help plan, guide and evaluate the Iranian educational reform was begun in 1974 and shall continue for five years. This project is part of the Unesco/World Bank educational planning project in Iran. The work on simulation models has inspired a new research programme on global modelling research in this field, which after addressing itself to world issues, is now focusing on regions and especially on constraints to development. The work of Unesco in this area seeks to bring results to the level of practicability, with planning in view. In that context close association has been established with the ISSC programme of conferences and symposia on global models. Besides making an intellectual input to some of these conferences, Unesco will run a series of workshops for training specialists from developing countries in methods of global modelling and in dynamic systems analysis.

Research period: 1973-1976. Research funds: $18,500.

(c) Evaluation

A meeting of experts was organized in 1974 to identify research needs in this field. In 1975, in addition to a survey of Indian experience in evaluation research and application, evaluation studies of a functional literacy project and of a family planning programme in India are being carried out. These research studies will be discussed by a workshop meeting in New Delhi in 1976, under the joint responsibility of the Indian Planning Commission and Unesco.

Research period: 1973-1976. Research funds: $52,000.

17. Apart from setting priorities and conducting research, there is also a problem of disseminating research results and establishing improved data bases and information sources in general. Discussions concerning research in the developing countries unavoidably become abstract if they do not take into account the necessary data base as well as the proliferation of small projects which acquire any cumulative weight nor lead to any systematic addition to the generally usable information stock. Storage, processing and quick retrieval of social science data, indispensable in any country, are particularly important for the developing countries. After all, the social scientists, responding to the tremendous challenge posed by the current transition of the Third World, have not long been engaged in gathering the most essential data. Every piece of reasonably scholarly information about any aspect of social change in the developing societies should therefore not be allowed to fall into oblivion. It might prove invaluable at a stage when a more theoretically-minded social scientist would pick it up and incorporate it into a meaningful conceptual framework.

The crux of the problem seems to be the above-mentioned absence of real institutional continuity in social science research in the developing countries. Alongside with the frequent changes of the directors and senior staff of research institutes, research plans are abandoned and, what is worse, research projects already under way and often even the exploitation of the research data for which all the empirical material is assembled ready to be processed. Almost all those who practise the social sciences is the developing countries complain constantly of lack of data, of unexplored fields, etc., but what is often overlooked is the immense quantity of data existing but still unexploited or only very partially exploited. In some institutes the problem consists not in the absence of data for processing but in the shortage of qualified staff to carry out this processing properly. What is needed in short for the developing countries, is the greater utilization and availability of archives of numerical and other data, especially as regards machine-readable files. This in turn depends on: the level of detail of the material stored and its ability to be disaggregated and subsequently reconstituted in other forms and for other purposes; the standardization of definition of terms and units of measurements; the retirement of material not in current demand to passive files in such a way that subsequent retrieval is possible if required for further analysis; the incorporation into data storage systems of indicators which would help in the assessment of the quality and nature of data; standard forms of description for individual data files; facilities for the international exchange of files, etc.

Research Councils have a particular responsibility for the overall national data organization. Their concern is - or should be - both the formulation of national information policy for the social sciences in a given country and practical steps taken towards the establishment of a satisfactory national system of information. The latter calls among others for: a national list and index of data archives available; a comprehensive and effective system of bibliographical control over all forms of recorded knowledge which are issued in that country; a comprehensive collection of indigenous forms of recorded knowledge, organized for use by social scientists; inter-library loan access for other countries to its own publications; records of researchers and of research progress, etc. Further, some of these Councils may well be drawn into the UNISIST framework (which is primarily a framework for co-ordinating and standardizing a wide range of information-based activities in all areas of science) to act as "national focal points" responsible for operational matters including the collection of information about operating systems. Such focal points exist already for the natural and technical sciences in several Asian, African, Arab and Latin American countries. Unesco, whose aim is to establish a generalized, universal and openly accessible system of exchange of social science information on a structural and continuing basis, can offer guidance and advice on the organization of national systems as well as on the design of suitable mechanisms for linkage of national with international systems. It can also, in co-operation with Member States, collect and disseminate information on bilateral and regional arrangements, particularly cross-national ones, for practical co-operation between information services in the social sciences and assist in organizing the training of information specialists in the social sciences (this is envisaged in the programme activities for 1976 by the Arab Centre in Cairo and the African Centre in Kinshasa).

V

18. It is proposed to close this paper with a review of research priorities in the developing regions, which were set by the competent regional social science organizations.

In Africa - The Council for the Development of Economic and Social Research in Africa (CODESRIA), established at a conference in Dakar in January 1973, which adopted a constitution of this regional body, created an executive committee and a permament secretariat under the direction of an executive secretary and set up several inter-disciplinary and international research groups to work on subjects which were given priority in African conditions.

In Asia - The Asian Association of Social Science Research Councils (AASSREC), set up at an Asian conference on social science training and research at Simla in May 1973. The research priorities, mentioned in the listing below are in fact proposals presented by the President of AASSREC for the second meeting of the association to be held at Tehran in October 1975, which is to adopt among others a programme and budget of AASSREC for 1976-1977; the Asian Association of Development Research and Training Institutes, established at a meeting which was held in Bangkok in July/August 1973. It was at this meeting that several research priorities were selected to be carried out by the international research groups.

In the Arab region - The Arab Educational, Cultural and Scientific Organization (ALECSO), which at a meeting held at Algiers in March 1973 on "Recognition of sociology in the Arab World" established several research priorities in the field of sociology; the Eighth Regional Conference of the Arab National Commissions for Unesco, held at Tunis in September 1973, chose also several research themes to be investigated in the Arab States.

In Latin America - The Latin American Faculty of Social Sciences (FLACSO), established in 1958 in Santiago (since then its activities have been de-centralized and are localized in Buenos Aires as well and plans have been adopted for further de-centralization) from the very beginning combined teaching and research. The priorities mentioned below are those of the Institute of Co-ordination of Social Research of FLACSO (ICIS) in Santiago; they are contained in an information of the Institute's activities in 1973-1974 presented to the Extraordinary Assembly of FLACSO in Quito in April 1975; the Latin American Social Science Council (CLACSO), created in 1967, with which some 60 institutions are associated has set a number of research groups to work on topics considered significant and relevant for Latin America.

The situation varies from one region to another as regards the character and number of bodies involved; the degree of advancement of research activities - whether this is merely a stage of establishing priorities or already conducting research, perhaps even diffusing its results; the geographical and financial scope; period of time destined for research, etc. Whatever the differences, a common feature of research in all the regions concerned is an effort to organize it within the framework of regional co-operation; to work on research projects according to priority established by specialists from a given region; to prepare a design on a regional basis which would enable cross-national comparative investigation and interpretation of results; to select a good number of typical countries where research could be conducted; to present a given process (or phenomenon) as an entity and to look at it from the viewpoint of all relevant social science disciplines. Consequently, as regards Unesco's research activity, only those topics will be included for comparison which were selected for execution within the regional programmes - as broad transnational and multidisciplinary schemes, relating to a given region as a whole. These are also research activities where a principle of equity and partnership in Unesco's doing with the Third World has been applied to the fullest. The research priorities were established on the spot by local scholars at regional meetings of specialists which were organized by Unesco; the research has a transnational and multidisciplinary character and is conducted by specialists coming from various countries and representing various social science disciplines in the region; resources being in short supply in the developing countries, the cost of research is borne by Unesco, with the hope that later on funds from national bodies, international agencies and private foundations might be forthcoming.

Here is the situation in the particular regions.

AFRICA

Research priority	CODESRIA	Unesco
1. Approaches to development planning	x	
2. Rural development	x	x
3. Urbanization		x
4. Industrialization and income distribution	x	
5. Economic co-operation and integration	x	
6. Problems of least developed countries	x	
7. Population policies and economic development	x	
8. Monetary problems	x	
9. Political studies	x	

ASIA

Research priority	AASSREC	AADRTI	Unesco
1. Development planning	x	x	
2. Employment and unemployment		x	
3. Urbanization	x	x	
4. Rural development (Green revolution)		x	
5. Income distribution		x	
6. Bureaucracy and national development	x		
7. Multi-ethnic societies	x		
8. Modern occupations			x
9. Universities and national development			x
10. Choice and adaptation of technology		x	

ARAB REGION

Research priority	National Commissions	ALECSO
1. Rural development	x	
2. Environment	x	
3. Population growth	x	
4. Administration		x
5. Industrialization		x
6. Emigration		x

Research priority		CLACSO	FLACSO
1.	Rural studies	x	
2.	Urban and regional development	x	
3.	Science, technology and development	x	x
4.	Integration and economic development	x	
5.	Population and development	x	
6.	Education and development	x	
7.	Dependency	x	
8.	State and society	x	
9.	Cultural development	x	
10.	Political studies	x	
11.	Employment and unemployment	x	
12.	Income distribution	x	
13.	Economic history	x	
14.	Law and society		x
15.	History and society		x

A synoptic table showing research priorities in the developing countries as a whole is given below. Some of the priorities have been grouped together and - occasionally - reformulated in a more comprehensive or simpler manner. The order in which the research priorities appear is arranged according to the frequency of their representation in various regions; it starts with the highest score and ends up with the lowest.

Research priority		Region where it appears			
		Africa	Asia	Arab Region	Latin America
1.	Rural development	x	x	x	x
2.	Education and development	x	x	x	x
3.	Urbanization and regional development	x	x		x
4.	Income distribution	x	x		x
5.	Population and development	x		x	x
6.	Development planning	x	x		x
7.	Employment and unemployment		x		x
8.	Economic co-operation and integration	x			x
9.	Science and technology		x		x
10.	Cultural development			x	x
11.	Modern occupations		x		
12.	Multi-ethnic societies		x		
13.	Environment			x	
14.	State, law and political behaviour				x
15.	Economic and social history				x

Out of 15 research priorities prevailing in the developing regions, two (rural development; and education and development) appear in all the four regions, three (urbanization and regional development; income distribution; and population and development) are represented in three regions (in various combinations, Africa being the only con-stans), five priorities can be found in two regions and five too in only one region. The most pertinent are, of course, these research priorities which appear most frequently. The fact that rural development, and education and development are of importance to all the regions concerned, should not come as a surprise. The developing countries are agrarian societies and likely to remain so for a long time to come. Agriculture and rural development in general are the most crucial areas and a major untapped potential for the development of most African, Asian, Arab and Latin American countries. The same is true, mutatis mutandis, of education. In addition to being a cultural and social force, it is now recognized as a basic factor in economic development. Very characteristically, both rural development and education are major concerns of Unesco. As regards the first scheme, resolution 18 C/10.1 (Analysis of problems and table of objectives to be used as a basis for medium-term planning (1977-1982)) recommends that, in activities which fall within Unesco's field of competence, the Organization should aim to accord particular attention to Unesco's contribution to "integrated rural development". Education and

the problems of how to relate educational systems to overall development needs, economic and social, are, by the very nature of Unesco's Constitution, at the core of the Organization's preoccupations.

It is equally understandable that the next research priorities - in terms of frequency - should be urbanization and regional development (constituting with rural development an integrated whole), income distribution (stemming from a concern about social equity), and population and development (the vicious circle of poverty and population pressure being one of the main obstacles on the road to balanced development). It is not proposed to make a detailed analysis of the research priorities in the developing countries as they appear in the table. However, one more remark seems in order. This is that the notion of development as a multi-faceted, integrated process is an in-built concept in and gives an overall framework to all the research pursuits in the developing regions. This is in fact the most frequently applied research priority. As said at the outset of this sub-chapter, regional research schemes have been the subject of comparison. Were the subject a true international comparison of research on the basis of a wide sample which included a form of regional representation (e.g. one, or at the most, two countries per region) the results would be quite different, particularly with regard to studies on multi-ethnic societies and socio-cultural aspects of environment, each appearing in the table only in one respective region.

Meeting on Inter-Regional Co-operation in the Social Sciences
(Paris, 23-27 August 1976)

PROGRAMME

Monday, 23 August

a. m.   Opening of the meeting by the Representative of the Director-General.

                        Election of Chairman, two Vice-Chairmen and Rapporteur.

            Topic I   Review of the state of the social sciences in different regions:

                        presentation and discussion of the regional papers (Africa, Arab region, Asia, Europe, Latin America);

                        discussion will be focused on the institutional aspects.

p. m.   Topic I   Review of the state of social sciences in different regions (continued).

Tuesday, 24 August

a. m.   Topic II   Trends towards the internationalization of the social sciences:

                        presentation and discussion of the paper prepared by the International Social Science Council (ISSC).

p. m.   Topic III   "Regionalization" of the social sciences:

                        specific features of social science research and teaching in each region;

                        general and particular aspects of the prevailing paradigms in the social sciences;

                        the extent to which the social scientists in the developing countries have succeeded in establishing the relevant or region-specific research priorities, methods of research or "models".

Wednesday, 25 August

a. m.   Topic III   "Regionalization" of the social sciences (continued).

p. m.   Topic IV   Co-operation between developing countries: constraints and possibilities.

Thursday, 26 August

a. m.   Topic V   Co-operation between the developed and developing countries: centre-periphery theory re-examined.

p. m.   Topic VI   Towards global co-operation:

                        the ultimate purpose;
                        the possibility of concerted action;
                        mechanisms for co-operation;
                        rôles of Unesco, regional bodies and NGO's.

Friday, 27 August

a. m.   Topic VI   Towards global co-operation (continued).

p. m.   Adoption of report.

                        Concluding session.

List of Participants

Participants

Professor Mpekesa Bongoy
Director
Centre for the Co-ordination of Social Science
    Research and Documentation in Africa south
    of the Sahara
(CERDAS)

B.P. 836
Kinshasa XI, Republic of Zaire

Professor Abdalla Bujra
Executive Secretary
Council for the Development of Economic and
    Social Research in Africa
(CODESRIA)

B. P. 3.186
Dakar, Senegal

Dr. Francisco Delich
Executive Secretary
Latin American Social Science Council (CLACSO)

Av. Callao 875 3°E
Buenos Aires, Argentina

Dr. Samy Friedman
Secretary-General
International Social Science Council

1 rue Miollis
75015 Paris, France

Professor S. Abou El Ezz
Member, Governing Board - Centre for Social
    Science Research and Documentation for the
    Arab Region

c/o National Centre for Social and Criminological
    Research,
Gezira P.O., Cairo, Arab Republic of Egypt

Dr. Lee Sang-Joo
Secretary-General
Association of Asian Social Science Research
    Councils (AASSREC)

c/o Korean National Commission for Unesco
B. P. Central 64
Seoul, Republic of Korea

Professor T. N. Madan
Head, Asian Research Centre

Institute of Economic Growth
University of Delhi, Delhi 7, India

Professor Adam Schaff
President of the Board of Directors,
European Co-ordination Centre for
    Research and Documentation in Social Sciences

Grünangergasse 2
B. P. 974
A-1010 Vienna I, Austria

Observers

Dr. D.V. McGranahan
Director
United Nations Research Institute for Social
    Development (UNRISD)

Palais des Nations
1211 - Geneva 10
Switzerland

Dr. Paul-Marc Henry
President
Development Centre
Organization for Economic Co-operation and
    Development (OECD)

Château de la Muette
2 rue André Pascal
75016 Paris, France

Mrs. V. di Giacomo
Development Centre
Organization for Economic Co-operation
   and Development (OECD)

Château de la Muette
2 rue André Pascal
75016 Paris, France

Dr. Arne Haselbach
Executive Secretary
European Association of Development Research
   and Training Institutes

c/o Vienna Institute for Development
Karntner Str. 25
A-1010 Vienna
Austria

Dr. Jean Masini
European Association of Development
   Research and Training Institutes

c/o Vienna Institute for Development
Karntner Str. 25
A-1010 Vienna
Austria

Dr. S. Mills
Director
European Co-ordination Centre for Research
   and Documentation in Social Sciences

Grünangergasse 2
B.P. 974
A-1010 Vienna I
Austria

Professor S. Abou El Ezz
ALECSO
President of the Institute of Arab Research
   and Studies

109 Tahrir Street
Dokki,
Cairo
Arab Republic of Egypt

Professor E. Oteiza
Visiting Fellow
Institute for Development Studies
University of Sussex
Former Executive Secretary
Latin American Social Science Council (CLACSO)

Institute for Development Studies
University of Sussex
Brighton, United Kingdom

Unesco Secretariat

Mrs. M. Hildebrandt
Assistant Director-General for the Social
   Sciences and their Applications

Unesco
Place de Fontenoy
75700 Paris

Mr. V. Mshvenieradze
Director
Division for International Development of
   Social Sciences

Unesco, Paris

Mr. J. Ziolkowski
Senior Programme Specialist
Division for International
Development of Social Sciences

Unesco, Paris

Mr. T. Uchida
Programme Specialist
Division for International
Development of Social Sciences

Unesco, Paris

Mrs. M. Paul-Aristy
Programme Specialist
Division for International
   Development of Social Sciences

Unesco, Paris

Meeting Documents

I. Working papers

    1.   Programme (SHC/76/CONF. 807/1)

    2.   General Information (SHC/76/CONF. 807/2)

    3.   Provisional List of Participants (SHC/76/CONF. 807/3)

    4.   Social Science Co-operation in Latin America: Professor Oteiza (SHC/76/CONF. 807/4)

    5.   Social Science Co-operation in Asia: Professor Roy (SHC/76/CONF. 807/5)

    6.   Social Science Co-operation in Europe: Professor Schaff (SHC/76/CONF.807/6)

    7.   Social Science Co-operation in Arab States: Professor Khalifa (SHC/76/CONF. 807/7)

    8.   Social Science Co-operation in Africa: Professor Bongoy (SHC/76/CONF. 807/8)

    9.   Social Sciences as a Global Enterprise, I.S.S.C. (SHC/76/CONF. 807/9)

    10.   Unesco, Priorities for Social Science Research in Developing Countries (unnumbered)

II. Background materials

    1.   European Co-operation in Development Research, Training and Documentation (Dr. A. Haselbach, E.A.D.I.)

    2.   Centre de Vienne, 1975.

[SS.76.XV.10 F]